THE
BOOK
LOVER'S
ALMANAC

THE
BOOK
LOVER'S
ALMANAC

A Year of Literary Events, Letters,
Scandals and Plot Twists

ALEX JOHNSON

To Mum and Dad
Wilma, Thomas, Edward and Robert

First published in 2023 by
The British Library
96 Euston Road
London NW1 2DB

British Library Cataloguing in Publication Data

A catalogue record for this publication
is available from the British Library

ISBN 978 0 7123 5424 0

Design and typesetting
by Goldust Design

Printed and bound
in the Czech Republic by Finidr

CONTENTS

INTRODUCTION

Almanacs have been bestsellers for thousands of years, rivalling even sales of the Bible at their height, and they are still incredibly popular today. For farmers, nature enthusisasts and astrologers, they provide affordable calendars of the past and predictors of the future. Essential and affordable guides, their contents often also include poetry and proverbs.

The almanac you have in your hands is less agricultural, but what it lacks in phases of the moon and tide times, it makes up for in 'On This Day' tales of duelling novelists, manuscripts going up in flames, and Sylvia Plath's culinary delights on Boxing Day.

Of course it includes important births, deaths and first editions/performances across each month. There are also key milestones, such as the first recorded female printer and the birth of the Kindle. And at the heart of the book are the moments that offer a daily glimpse behind the literary curtain. Here is James Joyce on a sightseeing bus tour of the Waterloo battlefield, Thomas Mann on a trip to Venice, E. M. Forster looking around caves in India.

Naturally there's literary snark, too. Charlotte Brontë comments on Jane Austen, Joseph Conrad judges Herman Melville, and Samuel Pepys has a rotten time at *A Midsummer Night's Dream*. And while it is the best of times for Sylvia Townsend Warner when she checks out her bank balance while doing some housework, it's certainly the worst of times for the thirteenth-century Icelandic writer and statesman Snorri Sturluson, who just checks out.

For each of the 366 days of the year (actually, there are 367 here …), there's an item of interest, from George Eliot's to-do list on 1 January to Louisa M. Alcott's advice on Christmas Day for a budding writer. Lee Child has a life-changing moment on 1 September, Franz Kafka has a fruitless one on 7 June, and John Masefield finishes writing *The Box of Delights* on 23 March 1935, at 5.36 p.m. precisely.

On the small screen Joey and Rachel swap their favourite novels, while Frasier dresses up as Geoffrey Chaucer. On the big one, Robbie gives Baby the literary key to his philosophy of life ('Make sure you return it, I have notes in the margin').

The beauty of this almanac is that you have no idea what you're going to come across next: George Orwell breaking his spade handle while gardening, Queen Victoria very nearly discovering *The Mystery of Edwin Drood*, or Dylan Thomas's decidedly mixed success as a best man.

There are many ways to read it – using family birthdays, systematically from 1 January to 31 December, haphazardly as it falls open – but I hope that whichever you choose, you find plenty to enjoy, and maybe something to lead you down more rabbit holes (see 4 July).

JANUARY

*No one ever regarded the First of January with
indifference. It is that from which all date
their time, and count upon what is left.*
'New Year's Eve' in *London Magazine* (1821) by Charles Lamb

Births
Stella Gibbons (5 January 1902)
J. D. Salinger (1 January 1919)
Gerald Durrell (7 January 1925)
Haruki Murakami (12 January 1949)
Nicholson Baker (7 January 1957)

Deaths
Frances 'Fanny' Burney, Madame d'Arblay (6 January 1840)
Astrid Lindgren (28 January 2002)
Joan Aiken (4 January 2004)
Ursula K. Le Guin (22 January 2018)
Fay Weldon (4 January 2023)

First published/performed
28 January 1813: *Pride and Prejudice* by Jane Austen
1 January 1818: *Frankenstein; or, the Modern Prometheus* by
Mary Shelley
5 January 1886: *Strange Case of Dr Jekyll and Mr Hyde* by Robert
Louis Stevenson
19 January 1950: *Pebble in the Sky* by Isaac Asimov
5 January 1953: *En attendant Godot* (*Waiting for Godot*) by Samuel
Beckett

1

1869: George Eliot makes a to-do list in her diary. 'I have set myself many tasks for the year,' she writes. 'I wonder how many will be accomplished? – a novel called "Middlemarch", a long poem on Timoleon, and several minor poems.' On 2 August, she notes: 'Began Middlemarch'.

1909: Marcel Proust's biographer George Painter estimates that on (or about) this day, Proust eats some toast soaked in tea that brings back many childhood memories and inspires the madeleine incident in his *Remembrance of Things Past*.

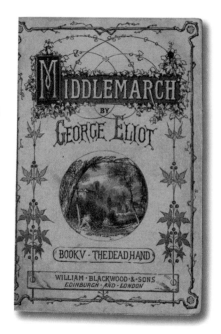

2

1897: Stephen Crane, riding high on the success of his American Civil War novel *The Red Badge of Courage* (1895), is shipwrecked. The SS *Commodore* on which he is travelling hits a sandbank off the coast of Florida and sinks. Crane spends a day in a lifeboat before being rescued. Undaunted, his first-hand account is front-page news in the national press on 7 January and the experience provides him with material for his short story 'The Open Boat', which he finishes in February.

1920: As he explains in his autobiography *In Memory Yet Green* (1979), Isaac Asimov chooses this day as his birthday because there's no record of his actual birthday and his parents could not confidently pinpoint it. He estimates it could actually have been any time between 4 October 1919 and this date.

3

The action of *Do Androids Dream of Electric Sheep?* by Philip K. Dick, first published in 1968, begins on this date in 1992, although later editions move it to 2021.

4

1853: Violinist Solomon Northup is granted his freedom, a dozen years after being abducted and sold into slavery. His memoir *Twelve Years a Slave* is published later in the year and becomes a bestseller.

5

1782: Poet William Cowper writes a letter to his friend William Unwin. Of Alexander Pope, he says: 'With the unwearied application of a plodding Flemish painter, who draws a shrimp with the most minute exactness, he had all the genius of one of the first masters. Never, I believe, were such talents and such drudgery united.' John Dryden fares a bit better: 'I admire Dryden most, who has succeeded by mere dint of genius, and in spite of a laziness and carelessness almost peculiar to himself.'

1821: Lord Byron mentions Sir Walter Scott in his diary: 'Wonderful man! I long to get drunk with him.'

1825: Alexandre Dumas père (born Dumas Davy de la Pailleterie), author of *The Three Musketeers*, fights a duel (swords, not pistols), aged twenty-three, after his clothing is disparaged by a soldier. Although he wins and is uninjured, some reports suggest his trousers fall down during the contest.

6

1482: Quasimodo is voted Pope of Fools in *The Hunchback of Notre Dame* (1831) by Victor Hugo during the annual Feast of Fools celebration.

7

1938: On his way home after going to the cinema with friends in Paris, thirty-one-year-old Samuel Beckett is pestered and then stabbed by a pimp called Prudent. He is taken to hospital where doctors manage to save his life (as did the thick overcoat he was wearing). Beckett later asks him why he did it, and Prudent replies: 'I don't know, I'm sorry.' Beckett drops the charges against him.

8

1981: Chilean writer Isabel Allende writes the letter to her dying grandfather which evolves into her novel *The House of the Spirits*. Allende then starts every new novel on 8 January, what she calls her 'sacred day'.

9

1845: This is what Charles Darwin borrows from the London Library on this day:

* *Journal of an Embassy to the Courts of Siam and Cochin-China* (1830) by John Crawfurd

* *Journal of a Residence in Norway during the Years 1834, 1835, and 1836, Made with a View to Inquire into the Moral and Political Economy of that Country and the Condition of Its Inhabitants* (1836) by Samuel Laing

* *The History of Greece*, volumes 2 and 3 (1784–1810) by William Mitford

* *Memoir of the Life and Public Services of Sir Thomas Stamford Raffles, FRS, Particularly in the Government of Java, 1811–1816, and of Bencoolen and its Dependencies, 1817–1824; with details of the commerce and resources of the Eastern Archipelago, and selections from his correspondence* (1830) by Lady Sophia Raffles

* *The Poetical Works of Robert Southey, Collected by Himself*, volume 4 (1845)

1924: Virginia Woolf buys a ten-year lease on 52 Tavistock Square in Bloomsbury. She will write *Mrs Dalloway* and set up the Hogarth Press here with husband Leonard (using the huge billiard room as storage space). The house is destroyed in October 1940 during the Blitz, a year after the Woolfs have moved to nearby 37 Mecklenburgh Square.

10

1748: This is the date of the first letter in Samuel Richardson's epistolary novel *Clarissa* or, to give it its full title, *Clarissa; or, The History of a Young Lady: Comprehending the Most Important Concerns of Private Life. And Particularly Shewing, the Distresses that May Attend the Misconduct Both of Parents and Children, In Relation to Marriage.* This first letter is from Miss Anna Howe to Clarissa Harlowe, the two being best friends:

'I am extremely concerned, my dearest friend, for the disturbances that have happened in your family. I know how it must hurt you to become the subject of the public talk: and yet, upon an occasion so generally known, it is impossible but that whatever relates to a young lady, whose distinguished merits have made her the public care, should engage every body's attention. I long to have the particulars from yourself; and of the usage I am told you receive upon an accident you could not help; and in which, as far as I can learn, the sufferer was the aggressor.'

1844: Having read Elizabeth Barrett's second collection of poems, Robert Browning writes to her at her home in Wimpole Street, London: 'I love your verses with all my heart, dear Miss Barrett ... and I love you, too.' They do not meet until later that year.

Dr Hastie Lanyon watches Hyde transform into his friend Jekyll in

Robert Louis Stevenson's *Strange Case of Dr Jekyll and Mr Hyde* (1886). The shock is too much for Lanyon and it kills him within a few days.

11

1879: Fifty thousand books and the original manuscript of the Coventry Mystery Plays with the Coventry Carol are destroyed in a huge fire at Birmingham Central Library. Only a very small part of the manuscript collection is saved, including a fifteenth-century illuminated manuscript, the Guild Book of Knowle, but most of the lending library volumes survive.

2007: J. K. Rowling completes the *Harry Potter* heptalogy in room 552 of the Balmoral Hotel, Edinburgh, marking the occasion by writing, 'Finished Writing Harry Potter and the Deathly Hallows in this room (552) on 11th Jan. 2007' on a marble bust in the room. She has been living and working there for six months to avoid distractions at home. In a tweet on this day in 2016 she writes: 'Finished Hallows 9 yrs ago today. Celebrated by graffiti-ing a bust in my hotel room. Never do this. It's wrong.'

12

1848: 'Why do you like Miss Austen so very much? I am puzzled on that point. What induced you to say that you would have rather written "Pride and Prejudice" or "Tom Jones", than any of the Waverley Novels? I had not seen "Pride and Prejudice" till I read that sentence of yours, and then I got the book. And what did I find? An accurate daguerreotyped portrait of a commonplace face; a carefully fenced, highly cultivated garden, with neat borders and delicate flowers; but no glance of a bright, vivid physiognomy, no open country, no fresh air, no blue hill, no bonny beck. I should hardly like to live with her ladies and gentlemen, in their elegant but confined houses. These observations will probably irritate you, but I shall run the risk.' Charlotte Brontë, letter to G. H. Lewes.

1895: In his notebook, Henry James notes that the archbishop of Canterbury, Edward White Benson, has told him a ghost story during

a teatime visit. It centres on evil servants in a country house who die after looking after two orphaned children and come back to haunt them. 'It is all obscure and imperfect, the picture, the story,' he writes, 'but there is a suggestion of strangely gruesome effect in it.' James turns it into his 1898 novella *The Turn of the Screw*.

1912: James Murray, busily editing the ongoing work of the *Oxford English Dictionary*, writes to the poet laureate Robert Bridges asking him about his use of the word 'Thwarteous' in his 1890 verse play *The Christian Captives* ('Satan did persuade our thwarteous king'). Bridges replies on this day: 'As I remember nothing about this word I think it best to say nothing.'

1997: The HAL 9000 computer goes online in *2001: A Space Odyssey* by Arthur C. Clarke (in the film, the year is 1992).

13

1535: Francis I moves to try to stop the spread of the Lutheran 'heresy' by introducing a statute banning printing and forcing bookshops to shut in France. He follows it on 28 December 1537 with the *Ordonnance de Montpellier*, which requires publishers to deposit their books in his own library before selling them to the public, thereby inaugurating the legal deposit system.

1898: Émile Zola publishes his 'J'Accuse' open letter about the Dreyfus Affair in the French newspaper *L'Aurore*, blaming the military for a cover-up over its conviction and imprisonment of Jewish officer Alfred Dreyfus four years earlier.

14

1689: Having finally returned home on 11 July 1687, the eponymous Robinson Crusoe gets itchy feet again and travels to Lisbon to sort out his financial affairs in Brazil. He heads home via Madrid, Pamplona, Toulouse, the Pyrenees (where he survives an attack by 300 ferocious wolves in heavy snow) and Paris, before heading on to Calais and arriving back in England again, in Dover, on this day.

15

1622: At his birth in Paris, French playwright Jean-Baptiste Poquelin – who will become better known by his pseudonym 'Molière' – is seen by one of the family's maids, who squeals 'Le Nez!' on seeing his large nose. This becomes his childhood nickname.

The eponymous Jane Eyre meets the unpleasant supervisor of Lowood School, Mr Brocklehurst, for the first time in Charlotte

Brontë's novel. 'It was the fifteenth of January, about nine o'clock in the morning: Bessie was gone down to breakfast; my cousins had not yet been summoned to their mama; Eliza was putting on her bonnet and warm garden-coat to go and feed her poultry, an occupation of which she was fond: and not less so of selling the eggs to the housekeeper and hoarding up the money she thus obtained.'

1907: Joseph Conrad declines to contribute a preface to a new edition of *Moby-Dick* for Oxford University Press. In his letter to publisher Humphrey Milford at OUP he writes: 'I am greatly flattered by your proposal; but the writing of my own stuff is a matter of so much toil and difficulty that I am only too glad to leave other people's books alone. Years ago I looked into *Typee* and *Omoo*, but as I didn't find there what I am looking for when I open a book I did go no further. Lately I had in my hand *Moby-Dick*. It struck me as a rather strained rhapsody with whaling for a subject and not a single sincere line in the 3 vols of it.'

16

1928: Thomas Hardy's ashes – minus his heart, which is (probably) buried in Stinsford, Dorset – are interred in Westminster Abbey's Poets' Corner. Pallbearers include writers A. E. Housman, Rudyard Kipling, J. M. Barrie, John Galsworthy, Edmund Gosse and George Bernard Shaw, as well as prime minister Stanley Baldwin (Kipling's cousin) and leader of the opposition Ramsay MacDonald. This is the first time Kipling and Shaw meet. According to Shaw's secretary Blanche Patch, Kipling 'shook hands hurriedly and at once turned away as if from the Evil One'. Shaw, who remarks on the organist's excellent performance of the funeral march from Handel's *Saul*, tells Patch later 'that he thought the arrangement was very bad stage-management as he was so much taller than Kipling'.

17

1956: Allen Ginsberg writes his stream of consciousness poem 'America', which he will include in his *Howl and Other Poems* collection published in November.

1967: John Lennon starts writing the song for the Beatles, 'A Day in the Life', after reading an article about the number of potholes in Blackburn, Lancashire (4,000 'or one twenty-sixth of a hole per person') in today's *Daily Mail*.

18

1939: W. H. Auden and Christopher Isherwood emigrate to the United States. Both become American citizens in 1946, Auden on 20 May, Isherwood on 8 November.

1914: There's a symbolic handing of the poetic baton at a lunch on this day which becomes known as the Peacock Meal. Six poets – W. B. Yeats, Ezra Pound, Thomas Sturge Moore, Richard Aldington, Victor Plarr and Frank Flint – drive down from London at the invitation of seventy-three-year-old bohemian poet Wilfrid Scawen Blunt (married to Lord Byron's granddaughter, Lady Anne Isabella King-Noel). At lunch at Blunt's home in West Sussex, they eat roast peacock (Yeats says it tastes like turkey) and roast beef, and then the younger poets give Blunt a marble box designed by the avant-garde sculptor Henri Gaudier-Brzeska. It has a nude female Egyptian figure carved on one side of it and is filled with the guests' own poems, none of which impresses Blunt, who describes the contents as merely 'word problems' and promptly turns the carved side towards the wall. Later they are joined by Blunt's neighbour Hilaire Belloc, and around 5 p.m. they drive back to London. Organised by Lady Augusta Gregory, once a lover of Blunt's, one of the main reasons for the dinner is that Ezra Pound – then working as Yeats's secretary – wants to meet every poet in England (though then poet laureate Robert Bridges turns down an invitation to the meal as he dislikes Blunt). In her book *Poets and the Peacock Dinner* Lucy Diarmid describes it as 'both a ritual of affiliation and a networking event', with half a dozen accounts of the meal published in journals and newspapers in England and the US, and photos of the occasion turning it into an early literary PR success for all involved. Indeed the networking is also of a romantic nature since Pound, Yeats and Blunt have a Bloomsbury-esque connection, with various lovers in common.

19

1853: Charlotte Brontë replies to a pharmacist named David Waldie who has written to say how much he has enjoyed *Jane Eyre*. At this point, she is still writing using a pseudonym and signs the letter 'C Bronte' as well as using masculine pronouns. 'The sincere affection of a reader's gratification is – I scarcely need to say – one of the much acceptable favours in which an author can be repaid for his labours,' she writes. 'I shall be glad if any future work of mine gives you equal pleasure to that you speak of having found in *Jane Eyre*.' The letter sells at auction in 2013 for more than £30,000.

1930s?–2009: On this day for many years, to celebrate Edgar Allan Poe's birthday in 1809, an anonymous figure arrives annually at the writer's grave. Dressed in black, with a white scarf and a wide-brimmed hat, they pour a measure of cognac, toast Poe's memory, then leave three roses on the grave and disappear. The Toaster's last appearance is in 2009 and their identity is never discovered, though it is believed that there has been more than one, since notes left at the grave become more controversial in later years. Earlier notes were often cryptic, such as 'Edgar, I haven't forgotten you,' while a later one criticises the French government for its role in the Iraq War.

20

1959: Sylvia Plath has her brother Warren around for dinner. She cooks roast beef, creamed spinach in broth and her signature pudding, lemon meringue pie.

1993: Maya Angelou recites her poem 'On the Pulse of Morning' at US President Bill Clinton's inauguration; she is the first woman and the first African American to do so.

2021: Amanda Gorman recites her poem 'The Hill We Climb' at US President Joe Biden's inauguration; at twenty-two years old she is the youngest poet to do so.

21

1919: Ernest Hemingway arrives back in the US after his involvement in the First World War. He is interviewed dockside on disembarking from the *Giuseppe Verdi* wearing his red satin-lined cape over his officer's uniform, by a reporter from the *New York Sun*. His not entirely accurate article appears under the headline 'Has 227 Wounds, But Is Looking for Job – Kansas City Boy First to Return from the Italian Front', and when the *Chicago Tribune* follows it up, the headline is 'Worst Shot-up Man in US on Way Home'. Hemingway is hopeful that the nurse whom he has met and fallen in love with in Milan, Agnes von Kurowsky, will follow him soon. But on 7 March she writes that she is now engaged to an Italian officer and Hemingway never sees her again.

1926: Vita Sackville-West composes a love letter to Virginia Woolf, written while travelling in Milan but posted in Trieste. 'I am reduced to a thing that wants Virginia,' she writes, saying how much she misses Woolf and admonishing her a little for her flowery phrasing in expressing emotion. This letter, she says, is 'really a squeal of pain'. Woolf replies five days later, gently defending her use of what Sackville-West calls her 'lovely phrases' and calling her 'a longeared owl and ass' to prove she's not always flowery. She adds that she misses her very much.

1939: W. B. Yeats writes his last poem, 'The Black Tower', a week before he dies. Towers have played an important symbolic part in his poetry: twenty-two years earlier he bought a medieval tower (Thoor Ballylee) in County Galway, which he has restored and used as a writing studio. On it he has mounted a plaque which reads:

I, the poet William Yeats
With old millboards and sea-green slates
And smithy work from the Gort forge
Restored this tower for my wife George;
And may these characters remain
When all is ruin once again.

2014: Shaun Bythell in his book *Diary of a Bookseller* notes that five customers come into the shop today and spend a total of £40.50. An afternoon customer asks him for a copy of Alfred Barnard's book *The Whisky Distilleries of the United Kingdom*. When Shaun tells him that happily there are five copies in stock, the customer snorts and leaves the shop. Later it starts snowing.

22

1925: D. H. Lawrence in a letter to Italian writer and critic Carlo Linati: 'Whoever reads me will be in the thick of the scrimmage, and if he doesn't like it – if he wants a safe seat in the audience – let him read somebody else.'

23

1605: English poet John Donne, born into a Roman Catholic family but later a convert to Anglicanism, is ordained a Church of England priest.

2015: The movie *The Boy Next Door* starring Jennifer Lopez opens. Early on in the film Noah, a lovestruck nineteen-year-old suitor, attempts to win Ms Lopez's affections by presenting her with a first edition of the *Iliad* which he has bought in a yard sale. It has a snazzy gold and blue cover and although Lopez's character Claire refuses to accept it because it must have cost a fortune, he nonchalantly tells her that he only paid a buck for it … The book in the film is not a prop but an 1884 edition of the Alexander Pope 1715 translation, printed and bound by Donohue & Henneberry of Chicago.

24

1684: Celebrated diarist John Evelyn enjoys a visit to the Frost Fair on the Thames, which has frozen over to a depth of 18 inches. 'The frost continues more and more severe, the Thames before London was still planted with booths in formal streets, all sorts of trades and shops furnished, and full of commodities, even to a printing press, where the people and ladies took a fancy to have their names printed, and the day and year set down when printed on the Thames: this humor took so universally, that it was estimated that the printer gained £5 a day, for printing a line only, at sixpence a name, besides what he got by ballads, etc.'

1922: Edith Sitwell performs her collection of poems *Façade: An Entertainment* at a private performance in her brother Osbert's home in Carlyle Square, London, with an instrumental accompaniment by William Walton. It is held in the L-shaped drawing room on the first floor and Edith recites using a kind of megaphone made out of papier mâché to add clarity. Both she and the performers are hidden behind a painted curtain with a large mask in the middle – Edith sticks the megaphone through its mouth to declaim. The first public performance is given on 12 June the following year in the Aeolian Hall, London.

1934: Between 10 a.m. and noon, John Masefield begins writing *The Box of Delights*, almost certainly in the garden office hut at his Boar's Hill home in Oxford. As well as the time, he notes 'Sparrows' and 'Cold'. He finishes it on 23 March 1935, at 5.36 p.m. precisely, recording that it is 'Stormy W'.

25

1640: Author of *The Anatomy of Melancholy* Robert Burton dies extremely close to the date he predicted when casting his own horoscope some years earlier. Consequently, there are rumours of suicide but these are not substantiated.

26

1901: Strangeways & Sons prints 250 copies of *The Tale of Peter Rabbit* with black-and-white illustrations and coloured frontispieces. One copy of this self-published, privately printed edition by Beatrix Potter contains the inscription:

In affectionate remembrance of poor old Peter Rabbit, who died on the 26th of January 1901 at the end of his 9th year ... whatever the limitations of his intellect or outward shortcomings of his fur, and his ears and toes, his disposition was uniformly amiable and his temper unfailingly sweet. An affectionate companion and a quiet friend.

27

1302: Condemned in his absence on trumped-up charges of corruption and embezzlement, Dante Alighieri is exiled from Florence on threat of being burned at the stake if he returns. During his exile he writes the *Divine Comedy*. His sentence is overturned in 2008.

1922: As snow is falling, Franz Kafka arrives late in the evening at the popular Czech winter resort Špindlerův Mlýn (then known as Spindelmühle) in a horse-drawn sleigh, and begins writing *The Castle*. The opening chapters reflect this arrival.

28

1728: Esther Johnson, the love of satirist and cleric Jonathan Swift's life, dies. Swift has hurried back to Dublin from visiting his old friend Alexander Pope in England to be with the woman he has known since childhood – and may have secretly married – but finds he cannot face being with her during her final moments (nor the funeral two days later on 30 January). She dies at 6 p.m., Swift is notified at 8 p.m., and at 11 p.m. he begins writing 'On the Death of Mrs Johnson', his short tribute-biography of the woman he dubbed Stella.

1913: During the morning, E. M. Forster visits the hill caves of Barabar in the North Indian state of Bihar. This experience inspires a key plot element in his 1924 novel *A Passage to India*. It has not been a happy trip to India for Forster, who is visiting his friend Syed Ross Masood, with whom he is in love, but who is engaged to be married – in a diary entry for 27 January Forster writes that it has been a 'long and sad day', perhaps the moment when he was rejected by Masood.

29

1845: 'The Raven' is published in the *Evening Mirror* in New York, the first time that its author Edgar Allan Poe has had his name attached to it in print.

30

1815: In August 1814, the first Library of Congress is destroyed when British troops capture Washington, DC and burn down the US Capitol, which holds the 3,000-volume collection. On this day, President James Madison approves an act of Congress to spend $23,950 on buying Thomas Jefferson's library of around 6,500 books, which he has offered to the nation to help rebuild the collection. In fact Jefferson's library is about twice as big as the one lost in the flames, and covers a wider selection of topics, even including cookbooks.

1933: Ezra Pound meets one of his heroes, Italy's dictator Benito Mussolini, at 5.30 p.m. and recites some drafts from his most famous work, the *Cantos*. Il Duce enjoys them. Pound also slips him a pamphlet expounding his thoughts on monetary polices. Il Duce ignores these. From this time onwards, Pound becomes increasingly anti-American and anti-Semitic, which will lead to charges of treason at the end of the Second World War and confinement in an insane asylum for more than a decade in Washington, DC.

1997: The *Friends* episode 'The One Where Monica and Richard Are Friends' airs. Joey and Rachel agree to swap favourite books, so Joey reads *Little Women* and Rachel tackles *The Shining* (which scares Joey so much he keeps it in the freezer). Joey enjoys *Little Women* but accidentally tells Rachel spoilers about *The Shining*. Rachel does the same, which depresses Joey until she makes up a happier version.

31

Today is the feast day of St John Bosco (1815–1888). Bosco was an Italian Catholic priest and prolific writer on religious subjects who also ran his own printing workshop where he trained up many apprentices. He is the patron of editors and publishers (plus juvenile delinquents and magicians). He was proclaimed a saint in 1949 by Pius XII.

1964: In the nick of time, Charlie Bucket finds the last gold ticket in *Charlie and the Chocolate Factory* by Roald Dahl.

FINAL WORDS

'Try to be forgotten. Go live in the country.
Stay in mourning for two years, then remarry,
but choose somebody decent.'
Alexander Pushkin (29 January 1837)

'By the Immortal God, I will not move. '
Thomas Love Peacock (23 January 1866)

'Take away those pillows. I shall need them no more.'
Lewis Carroll (14 January 1898)

'I love the rain. I want the feeling of it on my face.'
Katherine Mansfield (9 January 1923)

'Does nobody understand?'
James Joyce (13 January 1941)

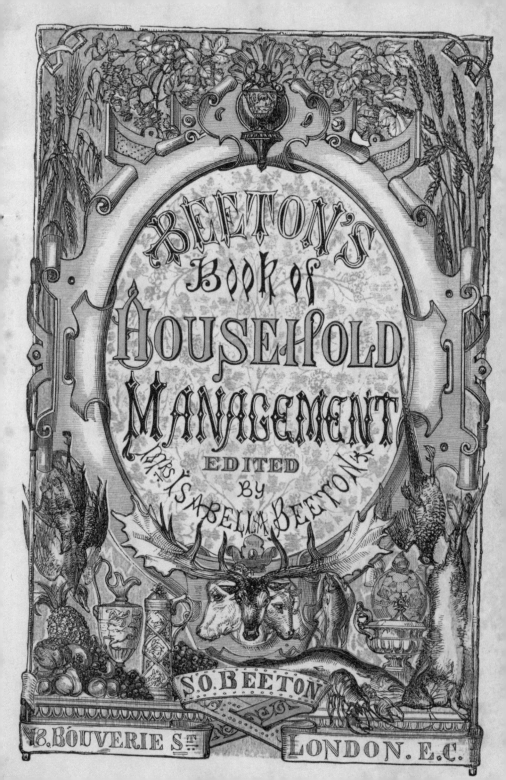

BEETON'S
BOOK of
HOUSEHOLD
MANAGEMENT

EDITED
BY
MRS ISABELLA BEETON

S.O. BEETON

18. BOUVERIE ST.

LONDON. E.C.

FEBRUARY

Good morrow, Benedick. Why, what's the matter
That you have such a February face,
So full of frost, of storm and cloudiness?
Don Pedro, Act 5, Scene 4, *Much Ado About Nothing*
(1598–9) by William Shakespeare

Births
Laura Ingalls Wilder (7 February 1867)
John Steinbeck (27 February 1902)
Georges Simenon (13 February 1903)
Patrick Leigh Fermor (11 February 1915)
Malorie Blackman (8 February 1962)

Deaths
Ann Radcliffe (7 February 1823)
Isabella Beeton (6 February 1865)
Umberto Eco (19 February 2016)
Harper Lee (19 February 2016)
Shirley Hughes (25 February 2022)

First published/performed
4 February 1826: *The Last of the Mohicans* by James Fenimore Cooper
4 February 1895: *The Importance of Being Earnest* by Oscar Wilde
2 February 1922: *Ulysses* by James Joyce (his fortieth birthday)
6 February 1937: *Of Mice and Men* by John Steinbeck
6 February 1939: *The Big Sleep* by Raymond Chandler

1

1884: The first part of the *Oxford English Dictionary* – or, to give it its full title 'A New English Dictionary on Historical Principles; Founded Mainly on the Materials Collected by the Philological Society' – sees the light of day. The ambitious project to record English language vocabulary from the twelfth century to the present had been expected to take ten years. After five they have reached 'Ant', at which point it is decided to publish the work thus far at a cost of 12*s* 6*d*, and then reconsider schedules and working practices.

1964: In Roald Dahl's *Charlie and the Chocolate Factory*, Willy Wonka takes the Golden Ticket winners on a tour of his industrial confectionery complex (though in the 1971 film it is inexplicably moved to 1 October). His instructions are simple – turn up at 10 a.m. sharp, up to two family guests allowed, don't forget to bring the ticket.

2

1585: Twins Hamnet and Judith, the children of William Shakespeare and Anne Hathaway, are baptised in Stratford-upon-Avon.

1709: Scottish sailor Alexander Selkirk, an inspiration for Daniel Defoe's novel *Robinson Crusoe*, is rescued after four years as a castaway on an uninhabited island in the Juan Fernández archipelago off the coast of Chile.

1902: During his visit to Italy, E. M. Forster falls *up* the steps at St Peter's in Rome and breaks his right arm (just as he is recovering from a sprained ankle in a previous fall). His mother looks after him for the rest of the month – washing, cooking and tending the many flea bites he gets on his arm – while visitors bring presents including buns, ivy from Cicero's villa, and a branch of mimosa.

3

1863: Samuel Clemens employs his pseudonym 'Mark Twain' for the first time in the *Territorial Enterprise*, a newspaper in Virginia, on a humorous piece of travel writing. It's not clear why he chooses the name. Clemens himself says he pinched it from a Mississippi riverboat captain, but it is also a phrase that indicates the depth of the water is safe enough for a riverboat to pass, and a signal in a bar that a customer wants two shots of whisky.

1931: The Arkansas state legislature passes a motion to pray for the soul of essayist and critic H. L. Mencken, known for his constant criticism of the South, and Arkansas in particular, which he has previously described as 'the apex of moronia' for its racism and 'Bible Belt barbarism' as well as being culturally dead.

1957: Noël Coward notes in his diary how much he is enjoying his annual rereading of all the works of E(dith) Nesbit, evoking many nostalgic memories of childhood. He describes her writing as 'so light and unforced', admires her humour and praises her narrative skills. Coward will be reading Nesbit's *The Enchanted Castle* on the day he dies (26 March 1973).

4

1818: Meeting at the house of poet Leigh Hunt, John Keats and Percy Shelley compete to see who can write the best sonnet about the Nile in fifteen minutes. Here is Keats's effort:

To the Nile
Son of the old Moon-mountains African!
Chief of the Pyramid and Crocodile!
We call thee fruitful, and that very while
A desert fills our seeing's inward span:
Nurse of swart nations since the world began,
Art thou so fruitful? or dost thou beguile
Such men to honour thee, who, worn with toil,
Rest for a space twixt Cairo and Decan?
O may dark fancies err! They surely do;
'Tis ignorance that makes a barren waste
Of all beyond itself. Thou dost bedew
Green rushes like our rivers, and dost taste
The pleasant sunrise. Green isles hast thou too,
And to the sea as happily dost haste.

This is what Hunt comes up with:

The Nile
It flows through old hushed Egypt and its sands,
Like some grave mighty thought threading a dream,
And times and things, as in that vision, seem
Keeping along it their eternal stands –
Caves, pillars, pyramids, the shepherd bands
That roamed through the young world, the glory extreme
Of high Sesostris, and that southern beam,
The laughing queen that caught the world's great hands.
Then comes a mightier silence, stern and strong,
As of a world left empty of its throng,
And the void weighs on us; and then we wake,
And hear the fruitful stream lapsing along
Twixt villages, and think how we shall take
Our own calm journey on for human sake.

And here is Shelley's attempt:

To the Nile
Month after month the gathered rains descend
Drenching yon secret Aethiopian dells,
And from the desert's ice-girt pinnacles
Where Frost and Heat in strange embraces blend
On Atlas, fields of moist snow half depend.
Girt there with blasts and meteors Tempest dwells
By Nile's aereal urn, with rapid spells
Urging those waters to their mighty end.
O'er Egypt's land of Memory floods are level
And they are thine, O Nile – and well thou knowest
That soul-sustaining airs and blasts of evil
And fruits and poisons spring where'er thou flowest.
Beware, O Man – for knowledge must to thee,
Like the great flood to Egypt, ever be.

Keats and Shelley gallantly agree that Hunt's is the best.

1857: Marian Evans signs her name *'George Eliot'* for the first time in a letter to her publisher, deciding it is a good way of hiding her gender and 'as a tub to throw to the whale in case of curious enquiries'. She says she has chosen George as it is her partner George Henry Lewes's first name, and Eliot because it is a 'good mouth-filling, easily-pronounced word'.

1938: Enclosed in a letter to Charles Furth at his publishers Allen & Unwin, who have already published *The Hobbit* (21 September 1937), J. R. R. Tolkien sends Chapter 1, 'A Long-expected Party', the opening of his sequel *The Lord of the Rings*. He also includes two lists of errata from *The Hobbit*, one sent to him by a young reader from Boston, Lincolnshire, the second put together by Tolkien's son Christopher, whom he has paid to find more mistakes at twopence a time.

5

1897: Marcel Proust fights a duel (pistols, not swords) on this rainy and cold day with writer and noted dandy Jean Lorrain after Lorrain suggests in a review of Proust's *Pleasures and Days* that the author may be having an affair with novelist Lucien Daudet. Incensed by this intrusion into his private life, Proust demands satisfaction and the two meet with their seconds in Paris's popular duelling spot, the forest of Meudon. At a distance of twenty-five paces, Proust shoots first. And misses. Lorrain shoots. And misses. Honour is satisfied, everybody goes home and there is a decent write-up of the duel in *Le Figaro*.

1941: Merchant ship the SS *Politician* is wrecked in rough weather off Eriskay, an island in the Outer Hebrides in Scotland, carrying nearly 30,000 cases of malt whisky and almost 300,000 ten-shilling notes. Evading the customs authorities' best efforts, islanders 'salvage' part of the ship's contents, some allegedly wearing their wives' dresses so that their own clothes are not contaminated by the ship's oil. Others bury bottles and sow oats on top to hide them. However, some islanders are caught and jailed for excise offences. The incident forms the basis of Compton Mackenzie's novel *Whisky Galore*, later made into a successful film in 1949.

1959: Earlier in the year, at one of Karen Blixen/Isak Dinesen's literary soirées, Blixen tells Carson McCullers that she's been really keen to meet not only McCullers but also E. E. Cummings, Ernest Hemingway and Marilyn Monroe. McCullers, quite pally with Marilyn, consequently hosts a lunch on this day at her home in Nyack, New York, and as a bonus Ms Monroe brings her husband, playwright Arthur Miller, along too. After their lunch of oysters, white grapes, champagne and soufflé, they dance together on a black marble tabletop. When Marilyn Monroe's personal library comes up for auction in 1999, it includes *The Ballad of the Sad Café* by McCullers.

6

1916: Artist and writer Marcel Duchamp writes four nonsense postcards – an artwork that becomes known as *Rendez-vous du Dimanche 6 Février*, one of what he calls his 'readymades' – to his neighbour to illustrate the limits of language. Although they are grammatically correct, the sentences are meaningless, and the text has no beginning or end.

7

1601: Robert Devereux, the Earl of Essex, pays Shakespeare's theatre company the Lord Chamberlain's Men forty shillings to perform the play *Richard II*. This focuses on the downfall of the monarch and is a prelude to a planned rebellion the following day. It all ends badly for Essex when the uprising collapses, and he is executed for treason on 25 February.

1857: After the publication of Gustave Flaubert's novel *Madame Bovary* in 1856 causes a major domestic incident, the author and his publisher Michel Lévy Frères go on trial for offending public and religious morality – both are acquitted on this day, with a meaningless judicial reprimand for Flaubert.

8

1841: Henry David Thoreau explains in his diary why he wants to keep one: 'My journal is that of me which would else spill over and run to waste, gleanings from the field which in action I reap. I must not live for it, but in it for the gods. They are my correspondent to whom daily I send off this sheet, post-paid. I am clerk in their counting-room, and at evening transfer the account from day-book to ledger. It is a leaf which hangs over my head in the path. I bend the twig, and write my prayers on it; then, letting it go, the bough springs up and shows the scrawl to heaven; as if it were not kept shut in my desk, but were as public a leaf as any in nature.'

1926: In Italo Calvino's short story about evolution, 'How Much Shall We Bet?', in his collection *Cosmicomics* (published 1965 in Italian, 1968 in English), Qfwfq and his friend Dean gamble on future events. Qfwfq tells him that on this day in 1926, twenty-two-year-old Signorina Giuseppina Pensotti will leave her house at number 18, Via Garibaldi, Santhia, in the province of Vercelli at 5.45 p.m., and asks him to guess if she will turn left or right.

9

1856: 'Query: when we are dreaming, and as often happens, have a dim consciousness of the fact and try to wake, do we not say and do things which in waking life would be insane? May we not then sometimes define insanity as an inability to distinguish which is the waking and which the sleeping life? We often dream without the least suspicion of unreality: "Sleep hath its own world," and it is often as lifelike as the other.' Lewis Carroll, diary entry

1911: An unsigned review in the *Morning Post* of *The White Peacock* on this day asks: 'What is the sex of D. H. Lawrence? The clever analysis of the wayward Lettie, surely a woman's woman, and the particular way in which physical charm is praised almost convince us that it is the work of a woman.' Lawrence writes to his sister Ida the same day that these ponderings 'amuse me highly'.

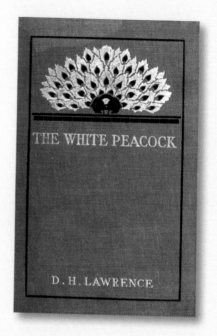

10

1863: Lewis Carroll finishes the text of *Alice's Adventures Under Ground*, but not the pictures until 13 September the following year.

11

1910: Ursula Todd is born in *Life After Life* by Kate Atkinson.

12

1884: Henry James visits French novelist Alphonse Daudet at his home in Paris and remarks that the average Frenchman is 'infinitely sharper in his observation' than the average American or Englishman.

1974: Aleksandr Solzhenitsyn is arrested for treason for writing *The Gulag Archipelago*. He is deported from the Soviet Union the following day.

1976: Mario Vargas Llosa punches Gabriel García Márquez in the face and floors him at a film premiere in Mexico City, shouting something along the lines of 'That's for what you said to Patricia'. Patricia is Vargas's wife, but despite numerous theories – mostly centring on

"The Queen of Hearts she made some tarts
    All on a summer day:
The Knave of Hearts he stole those tarts,
    And took them quite away!"

Now for the evidence," said the King, "and
  the sentence."

"No!" said the
  en, "first the
  tence, and then
  evidence!"

"Nonsense!" cried
  e, so loudly that
  ybody jumped,
  idea of having
  sentence first!

"Hold your
  e!" said the Queen.

"I won't!" said Alice, "you're nothing but a
k of cards! Who cares for you?"

At this the whole pack rose up into the
, and came flying down upon her: she gave
little scream of fright, and tried to beat
m off, and found herself lying on the bank,
h her head in the lap of her sister, who was
tly brushing away some leaves that had

Vargas's love life – the reason for the affray is never fully explained and the ongoing feud lasts until Márquez's death in 2014.

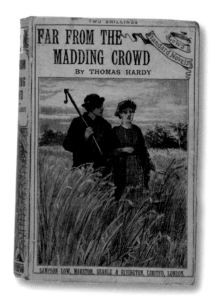

13

On the evening before Valentine's Day in *Far from the Madding Crowd* (1874) by Thomas Hardy, Bathsheba writes a card to local farmer Mr Boldwood – 'A rose is red / The violet blue / Carnation's sweet / And so are you' – and seals the envelope with the words 'Marry Me'. Penned in a fit of playfulness, the card will nevertheless have serious consequencs for both of them.

2000: The last *Peanuts* cartoon strip appears, a day after its writer Charles Schulz dies aged seventy-seven. Announcing his retirement due to his punishing publishing schedule, it features Charlie Brown on the telephone explaining that Snoopy, seen at his typewriter, is unavailable because he is writing.

14

1842: As soon as Charles Dickens arrives for his tour of the US and Canada he is greeted with what newspapers dub 'Bozmania', a nod to his pen name. 'I can do nothing that I want to do, go nowhere where I want to go, and see nothing that I want to see. If I turn into the street, I am followed by a multitude,' he writes to his friend the literary critic John Forster. Dickens has serious reasons for his trip, scrutinising conditions for prisoners and low-paid workers, visiting schools and libraries, and calling for international copyright laws. But there is also time for celebrations. Chief of these is a Valentine's Day event in the writer's honour in New York on this day which becomes known as the Boz Ball. The great and the good of the city descend on the Park Theatre to celebrate. 'The splendor of the interior of the Theatre cannot be adequately described,' writes George Lippard in the newspaper *Spirit of the Times* two days later. 'Flags, statues, festoons, wreaths of flowers, portrait of Boz, medallions of the President, fancy scenes, mirrors, chandeliers, tableau from Boz's works, &c., all combined to render the scene one of oriental enchantment. The supper was equal to that given by Cleopatra to Anthony.'

It is indeed. Writer Washington Irving is among the 3,000 diners who pay $5 for the night's entertainment, which extravagantly celebrates Dickens and his books. One contemporary account estimates that the great and the good consume 50,000 oysters, 10,000 sandwiches, 40 hams, 76 tongues, 50 rounds of beef, 50 jellied turkeys, 50 pairs of chickens and 25 of ducks, 2,000 fried mutton chops and '12 Floating Swans, a new device' (it's not clear what this is). Even the small fire that breaks out at one point does not halt the fun.

'Such was the tom-foolery of silly-minded Americans,' adds Lippard, 'and such the ridiculous homage paid to a foreigner, who will in all probability return home and write a book abusing the whole nation for the excesses of a few consummate blockheads.' This is almost exactly what the great Boz does in his *American Notes for General Circulation* which he will publish later this year, though he will also return for a triumphant reading tour of the US twenty-five years later.

1895: Cecily notes in her diary her engagement to Ernest (a full three months before she actually meets him) in *The Importance of Being Earnest* by Oscar Wilde.

1900: The events of *Picnic at Hanging Rock* by Joan Lindsay unravel (though the real calendar date for Valentine's Day in 1900 was a Wednesday, not a Saturday as in the book).

1989: Novelist and travel writer Bruce Chatwin's memorial service (he had died on 18 January) is held in the Greek cathedral of Saint Sophia in Moscow Road, London. Two hours before it begins, a fatwa on Salman Rushdie is announced on Radio Tehran by Ayatollah Khomeini, the spiritual leader of Iran. Rushdie is present at the service and sitting in the pew behind him is Paul Theroux, who leans forward and jokes: 'I suppose we'll be here for you next week.'

15

2003: The day of anti-war protests in London, during which Ian McEwan's novel *Saturday* takes place.

16

1833: Victor Hugo and Juliette Drouet start an affair that lasts half a century. Hugo also makes this the date in his novel *Les Misérables* on which Marius and Cosette get married.

2004: Edwin Morgan is appointed as the first makar, the national poet for Scotland.

17

1947: On the death of writer M. P. Shiel, the uninhabited Caribbean micronation Kingdom of Redonda

(of which he styled himself King Felipe I) passes to the London poet John Gawsworth (otherwise known as King Juan I).

1952: Ian Fleming begins writing his first James Bond novel, *Casino Royale*, on his typewriter at his summer home Goldeneye, in Jamaica. That first morning he knocks out 2,000 words and finishes the 62,000-word manuscript almost exactly a month later on 18 March.

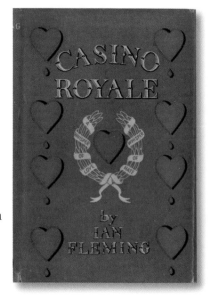

1992: After an interview, Philip K. Dick complains that his eyesight is worsening and is told to go to a hospital straight away. He does not, suffers a stroke, and is found unconscious at his home on February 18. He dies on 2 March in hospital, four months before *Blade Runner*, an adaption of his novel *Do Androids Dream of Electric Sheep?*, is premiered (see 3 January).

18

1965: The televised motion at the Cambridge Union this evening is 'The American Dream is at the expense of the American Negro'. Proposing is novelist and civil rights campaigner James Baldwin. 'I pick the cotton and I carry it to market, and I built the railroads. Under someone else's whip. For nothing,' he says. 'For nothing.' Opposing is the right-wing intellectual William F. Buckley Jr. Baldwin wins the vote by a significant margin, 544 to 164.

19

Bruce Wayne, aka Batman, is born.

20

1909: Italian poet Filippo Marinetti publishes his 'The Founding and Manifesto of Futurism' in French newspaper *Le Figaro*. 'Literature', says the manifesto, 'has hitherto glorified thoughtful immobility, ecstasy and sleep; we shall extol aggressive movement, feverish insomnia, the double quick step, the somersault, the box on the ear, the fisticuff.'

21

1904: Spending some time in Paris, Arnold Bennett notes in his journal that he is leading quite a solitary life, 'which is good for work but not for my nerves'. He thinks he needs more society, or, to be more exact, 'female society', or, to be even more exact, a 'sympathetic' woman. The result is that he has written 12,500 words during the preceding week.

22

1983: The play *Moose Murders* opens at the Eugene O'Neill Theatre on Broadway. A humorous whodunnit by Arthur Bicknell, it is not, to put it mildly, well received and also closes on this day. *New York Times* theatre critic Frank Rich does not mince his words, calling it 'the worst play I've ever seen on a Broadway stage'.

23

1455: The commonly accepted, but not factually proven, day when Johannes Gutenberg finishes printing his first Bible in Mainz,

Germany. Gutenberg's earliest definite printing is 22 October 1454, an indulgence for Pope Nicholas V.

24

1809: London's Drury Lane Theatre, co-owned by playwright and MP Richard Brinsley Sheridan, burns down. Sheridan watches the flames rise from the safety of a nearby pub, and when asked why he is so phlegmatic, replies: 'A man may surely take a glass of wine by his own fireside.' It reopens on 10 October 1812.

1852: Nikolai Gogol burns most of the second section of his novel *Dead Souls*. It's not clear why – theories include unhappiness with its progress, worries about its potential irreligious aspects and just plain accident. He dies shortly afterwards, on 4 March.

25

1954: William Golding's *Lord of the Flies* becomes the book's title after much to-ing and fro-ing between the author and his editor Charles Monteith. Discarded titles include 'Strangers from Within', 'Let's Play Islands' and 'Fun and Games'.

1956: Sylvia Plath meets Ted Hughes for the first time at a party in Cambridge. Recovering from a severe hangover the following day, she notes the immediate mutual attraction in her diary – their kissing unclips her earrings and leaves his cheek covered in blood where she bites him.

Today is the annual World Bookmark Day. The organisers' aim is 'to bring attention to bookmarks, the quiet companion of readers'.

26

Third Age 3019 or Shire Reckoning 1419: After an argument with Frodo, the Fellowship disbands as Boromir dies failing to protect Merry and Pippin from a band of orcs in *The Two Towers*, the second part of J. R. R. Tolkien's *The Lord of the Rings*.

1926: Graham Greene is received into the Roman Catholic Church and chooses St Thomas the Doubter as his confirmation saint, not Thomas Aquinas, as he explains to the priest during the ceremony.

27

1729: Poet John Byrom (the man who coins the phrase 'Tweedledum and Tweedledee') is also the inventor of a very popular system of shorthand widely used in the eighteenth century, as his diary entry for this day indicates: 'Called upon Mr Stanley, he began, paid five guineas, and promised no soul living should see it but himself; I showed him the way of coming at the alphabet, and left him to blunder by himself, and appointed to call on him to-morrow at nine.'

28

1571: Statesman, philosopher and essaysist Michel de Montaigne retires from public service and what he calls 'the slavery of the court'

to dedicate himself to reading and writing in the book tower of his castle near Bordeaux.

1910: British poet A. E. Housman replies to American poet and editor Witter Bynner, who has asked when more of his poems will be forthcoming: 'The other day I had the curiosity to reckon up the complete pieces, printed and unprinted, which I have written since 1896, and they only come to 300 lines, so the next volume appears to be some way off. In barrenness, at any rate, I hold a high place among English poets, excelling even Gray.'

1995: *The Diary of Bridget Jones* by Helen Fielding first appears as a column in the *Independent* newspaper. At this point Bridget weighs 8 st 13 lb, and consumes 2 units of alcohol, 7 cigarettes and 3,100 calories (poor).

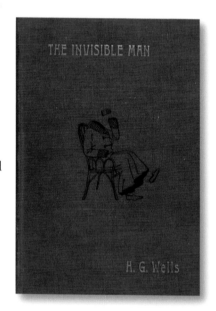

29

Griffin arrives in Iping at the start of H. G. Wells's *The Invisible Man* (published 1897).

FINAL WORDS

'I can feel the daisies growing over me.'
John Keats (23 February 1821)

'So, this is death. Well!'
Thomas Carlyle (5 February 1881)

'I loved you and did not cheat on you once,
even in my thoughts.'
Fyodor Dostoyevsky (9 February 1881), to his wife Anna

'So here it is at last, the distinguished thing.'
Henry James (28 February 1916)

'Even amidst fierce flames the golden
lotus can be planted.'
The headstone of Sylvia Plath (11 February 1963)

THANK YOU, JEEVES

P. G. WODEHOUSE

MARCH

March, master of winds, bright minstrel and marshal
of storms that enkindle the season they smite.
'March: An Ode' (1888) by Algernon C. Swinburne

Births
Dr Seuss/Theodor Seuss Geisel (2 March 1904)
Octavio Paz (31 March 1914)
Dick King-Smith (27 March 1922)
Elizabeth Jane Howard (26 March 1923)
Gabriel García Márquez (6 March 1927)

Deaths
Stendhal/Marie-Henri Beyle (23 March 1842)
Charlotte Brontë (31 March 1855)
Louisa May Alcott (6 March 1888)
Walt Whitman (26 March 1892)
Derek Walcott (17 March 2017)

First published/performed
26 March 1830: *The Book of Mormon*, attributed to Joseph Smith
16 March 1831: *Notre-Dame de Paris* (*The Hunchback of Notre Dame*)
by Victor Hugo
16 March 1850: *The Scarlet Letter* by Nathaniel Hawthorne
16 March 1934: *Thank You, Jeeves* by P. G. Wodehouse
21 March 1948: *Atómstöðin* (*The Atom Station*) by Halldor Laxness

1

1925: In *The Call of Cthulhu* by H. P. Lovecraft, an excited Henry Wilcox shows Professor Angell the intriguing, and still damp, clay bas-relief he made the previous night 'in a dream of strange cities'.

2

1909: At the Paddington Registry Office in London, Katherine Mansfield, wearing black and pregnant by a former lover, marries George Bowden. He is a decade older than her and a music teacher. She then has a change of heart and leaves him that evening before the marriage can be consummated. They divorce nine years later.

3

1875: Georges Bizet's opera *Carmen*, based on a novella by Prosper Mérimée, opens in Paris at the Opéra-Comique. It shocks the audience and outrages the critics with its amoral heroine. Bizet dies shortly afterwards on 3 June, aged thirty-six, on his wedding anniversary.

4

1866: In *A Princess of Mars* by Edgar Rice Burroughs (the first in his Barsoom series), John Carter and his friend John Powell travel to a gold mine in Arizona but are attacked by Native Americans. Powell is killed and Carter hides in a cave from where he is mysteriously transported to Mars. After numerous adventures, twenty years later Carter dies on Earth on the same day as he was whisked to Mars – leaving strange burial instructions to his nephew ...

1881: Sherlock Holmes gets the first case that is recorded by Watson in *A Study in Scarlet* (1887) by Arthur Conan Doyle. 'I rose somewhat earlier than usual,' writes the good doctor, 'and found that Sherlock Holmes had not yet finished his breakfast.'

1952: Ernest Hemingway finishes writing *The Old Man and the Sea* and tells his editor Wallace Meyer, 'I know that it is the best I can

write ever for all of my life,' adding that he hopes it will prove to people that his writing career is not over.

5

1839: Charlotte Brontë writes to Rev. Henry Nussey, brother of her friend Ellen, politely declining (she calls it a 'decided negative') his marriage proposal. 'I have no personal repugnance to the idea of a union with you,' she writes, but explains that 'I am not this serious, grave, cool-headed individual you suppose – You would think me romantic and eccentric – you would say I was satirical and severe.' Nussey does not take it personally and they stay on friendly terms.

1933: The young Judith Kerr, her brother Michael and her mother Julia escape from Nazi Germany over the border into Switzerland. Waiting for them is Kerr's father Alfred, a theatre critic and outspoken opponent of the Nazi regime, who has already fled the month before (14 February).

1977: Eighteen-year-old Kate Bush writes the song 'Wuthering Heights' late this evening, stimulated by watching a BBC adaption of the novel by Emily Brontë, with whom she coincidentally shares a birthday (30 July 1818 and 1958 respectively).

2006: Margaret Atwood launches her LongPen at the London Book Fair. It is a remote-controlled pen produced by Unotchit ('You-No-Touch-It') that means writers can sign books without having to be present at a book signing. Though some authors express disquiet, Atwood says: 'I think of this as a democratising device … You cannot be in five countries at the same time. But you can be in five countries at the same time with the LongPen.' After a brief technical hitch, she signs her collection of short stories *The Tent* for Nigel Newton, chief executive of her British publisher, Bloomsbury, writing on an electronic pad which relays the signature via two metal arms holding a pen. Her dedication is: 'For Nigel, with best wishes, Margaret Atwood.'

6

1834: Thomas Carlyle gets a nasty shock when his friend John Stuart Mill pays him a call at his home in Cheyne Walk, London, this evening. Carlyle has lent the first volume of his work in progress, a history of the French Revolution, to Mill, who explains he in turn has lent it to a friend whose maid has accidentally used it to light a fire and burnt the entire manuscript. Mill is hugely apologetic, but Carlyle is remarkably phlegmatic – indeed he hangs on to the burnt remains – and rewrites it from scratch, even though he has already thrown away all his notes. The book is published three years later.

1876: Walt Whitman replies to Bram Stoker after receiving an effusive fan letter from the man who will write *Dracula* twenty years later:

Your letters have been most welcome to me – welcome to me as Person, & then as Author – I don't know which most – You did well to write to me so unconventionally, so fresh, so manly, & so affectionately too. I too hope (though it is not probable) that we shall one day personally meet each other. Meantime I send you my friendship & thanks.

My physique is entirely shatter'd – doubtless permanently – from paralysis & other ailments. But I am up & dress'd, & get out every day a little – live here quite lonesome, but hearty, & good spirits.

Write to me again.

1935: Louisa Durrell and her children Gerald, Leslie and Margaret ('Margo') set sail for Corfu from Tilbury, Essex on board the SS *Hakone Maru*, a Japanese cargo freighter. The other sibling, Lawrence, has already left Tilbury on 2 March with his wife Nancy, heading for Corfu via Naples, on the SS *Oronsay*. Lawrence arrives on 14 March, the others on 28 March.

7

1912: Captain Robert Falcon Scott and his fellow explorers are heading home from the South Pole, having been beaten to it by Roald Amundsen's expedition. In his diary he writes that the feet of his comrade Titus Oates are looking bad. 'He is wonderfully brave. We still talk of what we will do together at home … One feels that for poor Oates the crisis is near, but none of us are improving.' Ten days later, Oates tells the others, 'I am just going outside and may be some time.' Scott notes: 'He went out into the blizzard and we have not seen him since.'

8

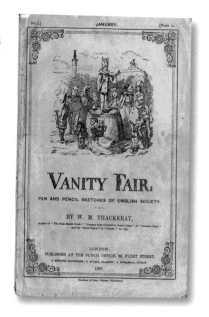

1978: Douglas Adams's *The Hitchhiker's Guide to the Galaxy* is first broadcast on BBC radio. The *Radio Times* calls it an 'epic adventure in time and space including some helpful advice on how to see the Universe for less than 30 Altairian dollars a day'.

2001: Astronaut Susan Helms goes into space on a 163-day mission to the International Space Station. She is allowed to pack ten paperbacks, and chooses a variety of classics (including *Gone with the Wind, Vanity Fair* and *War and Peace*), a couple of Russian detective novels and *The Third Wave* by Alvin Toffler.

2003: On International Women's Day, at an anti-war rally in the days running up to the invasion of Iraq, Alice Walker (author of *The Color Purple*) and twenty-six other women including writers Maxine Hong Kingston (author of *The Woman Warrior*) and Terry Tempest Williams are arrested as they protest peacefully outside the White House. Walker will write about the experience in her essay 'We Are the Ones We Have Been Waiting For'.

2015: It's the first airing for the BBC's new television series of the *Poldark* novels by Winston Graham, the original series having first been transmitted in 1975.

9

1870: Queen Victoria meets Charles Dickens at a private audience. In her diary she mentions that he was 'very agreeable, with a pleasant voice & manner', the two of them standing as they chat, although the monarch leans on a sofa. They discuss his reading tours, the nature of Americans, English class divisions and what he is currently working on. This is in fact his unfinished *The Mystery of Edwin Drood*. Indeed, the queen misses an opportunity to find out exactly how it would end, since Dickens has told her adviser Arthur Helps that he would be happy to tell her all about the plot and his plans. Apparently the queen is happy to wait to find out.

10

1943: Anne Frank writes in her diary about the Allied bombing of Amsterdam and the anti-aircraft gun response which is stopping her sleeping.

11

1923: In a letter to his patron Harriet Weaver, James Joyce says that he has just begun 'Work in Progress', which will namechange into *Finnegans Wake*. He says he has written two pages, the first he has completed since the final 'Yes' of *Ulysses*. He quotes to her the Italian saying 'Il lupo perde il pelo ma non il vizio', the English equivalent of which is 'The leopard can't change his spots'. This first passage is a draft of the 'King Roderick O'Conor' section.

12

1901: Andrew Carnegie offers New York City $5.2 million to build dozens of branch libraries, the largest single grant in his multi-million-dollar campaign to build libraries in a dozen countries.

1975: After twenty-eight years of incarceration, Andy Dufresne make his ingenious escape from Shawshank prison in Stephen King's novella *Rita Hayworth and Shawshank Redemption* (1982).

13

1602: John Manningham, a law student at Middle Temple in the Inns of Court, London, recounts in his diary a humorous story about Shakespeare …

'Vpon a tyme when Burbidge played Richard III. there was a citizen grone soe farr in liking with him, that before shee went from the

play shee appointed him to come that night vnto hir by the name of Richard the Third. Shakespeare ouerhearing their conclusion went before, was intertained and at his game ere Burbidge came. Then message being brought that Richard the Third was at the dore, Shakespeare caused returne to be made that William the Conqueror was before Richard the Third. Shakespeare's name William.'

14

1858: Louisa May Alcott's sister Lizzie/Beth dies. 'My dear Beth died at three in the morning after two years of patient pain,' she writes. 'Last week she put her work away, saying the needle was too heavy … Saturday she slept, and at midnight became unconscious, quietly breathing her life away till three; then, with one last look of her beautiful eyes, she was gone.' As she dies, Louisa, her mother and the doctor are at the bedside and all notice a kind of light mist rising from Beth's body as she dies, floating up into the air, then disappearing.

15

1820: Lord Byron is rather disparaging in a letter to essayist and novelist Isaac Disraeli about poet John Keats. Comparing him to his Lake District peers, William Wordsworth and Samuel Taylor Coleridge, he calls him 'a tadpole of the Lakes', a comment he comes to regret on Keats's early death less than a year later, at which point he describes him as a 'genius' and 'a loss to our literature'.

16

1949: Dorothy L. Sayers writes to Josephine Tey, fresh from her success the previous year with her mystery *The Franchise Affair.*

Sayers is honorary secretary of the Detection Club, formed in 1930 by herself and a Who's Who of British mystery writers including Baroness Emma Orczy, G. K. Chesterton, Agatha Christie and E. C. Bentley. She tells Tey that she has been elected as a member by secret ballot, adding that the club's sole purpose is 'mutual assistance, entertainment, and admiration'. She wonders if Tey would like to attend an initiation ceremony at their May meeting.

Tey, who lives in Inverness, replies three days later that she is bowled over by the invitation, but that she doesn't want to make any kind of speech and can't make the May date anyway. At the end of the month, Sayers responds that the speech issue is no problem, but Tey nevertheless never makes it to a club meeting or dinner.

The club survives today, along with its oath, 'Do you promise that your detectives shall well and truly detect the crimes presented to them using those wits which it may please you to bestow upon them and not placing reliance on nor making use of Divine Revelation, Feminine Intuition, Mumbo Jumbo, Jiggery-Pokery, Coincidence, or Act of God?'

Today is Lithuania's *Knygnešio diena or* Day of the Book Smugglers, chosen because it is also the birthday (in 1846) of Lithuanian newspaperman Jurgis Bielinis. During the Russian annexation of the country, when official policy was to replace all Latin alphabet books with Cyrillic ones, Bielinis put together an underground network to smuggle in banned Lithuanian books and distribute them around the country. Smugglers who were caught faced fines and exile to Siberia, or being shot. The ban officially lasted from 1864 to 1904, during which time millions of books were smuggled in, helping to preserve the Lithuanian language. There is a statue dedicated to 'The Unknown Book Smuggler' in the country's former capital, Kaunas.

17

1951: Dennis the Menace debuts in *The Beano* (the issue is dated today, though was on sale from 12 March, the same day that – entirely coincidentally – a different Dennis the Menace cartoon strip first appeared in more than a dozen newspapers in the US). In this first outing, Dennis goes for a walk in the park with his father and their dog, he repeatedly ignores signs to 'Keep Off the Grass', and his father eventually removes the lead from the dog and puts it on his son. Dennis takes over the *Beano* cover slot on 14 September, 1974.

18

1828: Sir Walter Scott on another attack of depression: 'I was sorely worried by the black dog this morning, that vile palpitation of the heart – that *tremor cordis* – that hysterical passion which forces unbidden sighs and tears and falls upon a contented life like a drop of ink on white paper which is not the less a stain because it conveys no meaning. I wrought three leaves, however, and the story goes on.'

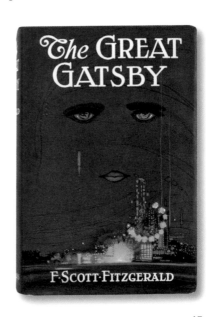

19

1925: F. Scott Fitzgerald in Paris cables his editor Max Perkins saying he's really keen to call his forthcoming book *Under the Red, White and Blue*, but it's too late to change it, so on publication day on April 10 it comes out as *The Great Gatsby*. Other previous suggestions that Perkins headed off have included *Trimalchio*, *Trimalchio in West Egg*, *Among Ash Heaps and Millionaires*, *On the Road to West Egg*, *The Gold-Hatted Gatsby* and *The High-Bouncing Lover*.

20

1928: Orlando gives birth to a son at 3 a.m. in Virginia Woolf's eponymous novel. This is also the date when Woolf finishes writing the book and writes to Vita Sackville-West, to whom the book is dedicated: 'Did you feel a sort of tug, tug, as if your neck was being broken on Saturday last at five minutes to one?' Naturally Sackville-West gets a copy when it is published on 11 October 1928, the date on which the novel ends at the last stroke of midnight.

21

1868: Nautilus reaches the South Pole in *Twenty Thousand Leagues under the Sea* (1870) by Jules Verne.

"'In 1868, on this 21st day of March, I myself, Captain Nemo, have reached the South Pole at 90°, and I hereby claim this entire part of the globe, equal to one-sixth of the known continents."

"In the name of which sovereign, Captain?"

"In my own name, sir!"

So saying, Captain Nemo unfurled a black flag bearing a gold 'N' on its quartered bunting. Then, turning toward the orb of day, whose last rays were licking at the sea's horizon: "Farewell, O sun!" he called. "Disappear, O radiant orb! Retire beneath this open sea, and let six months of night spread their shadows over my new domains!'"

22

Cecily breaks off her engagement with Ernest (two months before actually meeting him in person) in *The Importance of Being Earnest* (1895) by Oscar Wilde. 'To-day I broke off my engagement with Ernest,' she writes. 'I feel it is better to do so. The weather still continues charming.' The engagement has been settled for a month

(see 14 February) and she forgives him before the week is out.

23

1944: American novelist Dawn Powell reflects in her diary on the importance to a writer of 'escaping into solitude' and compares it to the feeeling she had as a child when clambering up into the attic or in a treetop 'where I was alone with a sharp pencil and notebook'.

24

1812: Lord Byron meets Lady Caroline Lamb for the first time at a dinner party, a couple of days after seeing her from afar at a soirée when she notes that her immediate impression on seeing Byron is that he was 'mad – bad – and dangerous to know.' After they meet today, she invites him to a morning reception at her house the following day – the date when Byron will also meet his future wife, Annabella – and they soon start a scandalous six-month affair.

25

1895: George Bernard Shaw, the American writer Frank Harris and Oscar Wilde's lover Lord Alfred Douglas meet Wilde at the Café Royal in London. Wilde is considering a lawsuit against the Marquess of Queensberry (Douglas's father) for criminal libel and asks Harris to appear for him in court. Harris argues that the lawsuit is a big mistake and could backfire terribly. Shaw agrees. Douglas contends that they should be supporting Wilde if they are real friends, and then leaves with Wilde. Wilde goes on to lose the case, is consequently convicted of gross indecency, goes to prison for two years, sees his marriage go up in smoke (see 26 March), goes into exile in France and suffers declining health until his death in 1900.

1957: As soon as they arrive after being printed in England, more than 500 copies of Allen Ginsberg's poem *Howl* are seized by US Customs for obscenity. Or as the Collector of Customs, Chester MacPhee, puts it: 'The words and the sense of the writing is obscene … you wouldn't want your children to come across it.' The books are released when the US Attorney decides not to go ahead with a prosecution, but on 3 June City Lights publisher Lawrence Ferlinghetti is arrested for selling it in his San Francisco bookshop. Ferlinghetti successfully defends the case, which is dismissed by California State Superior Court Judge Clayton Hall on 3 October: he rules that the poem is of 'redeeming social importance'.

1959: Tony Benn flies to Edinburgh to make a film with writer Compton Mackenzie, author of *Whisky Galore*. They get on very well and Mackenzie shows him around the house, including a basement where he is, perhaps surprisingly, about to open a ladies' hairdressing salon. He also explains his daily writing routine to Benn: get up after lunch, get dressed, start work after tea at 4 p.m., dinner at 7 p.m., watch television 8–10 p.m., work again 10 p.m.–2 a.m., then to bed to read and do crosswords until 4 a.m.

26

1897: Constance Wilde, Oscar's wife, writes to her brother from Italy about her husband's arrest and imprisonment: 'I think his fate is rather like Humpty Dumpty's, quite as tragic and quite as impossible to put right.' She says it will be impossible for them to live together again.

27

1802: After sitting down to write at breakfast, William Wordsworth completes the first four stanzas of his poem 'Intimations of Immortality from Recollections of Early Childhood'. Highlights of the finished poem include the acknowledgement that the early hours of 'splendour in the grass' cannot be recaptured.

1977: Woody Allen's Oscar-winning film *Annie Hall* premieres at the Los Angeles Film Festival. On a visit to a bookshop, Allen's character Alvy buys two books for Annie, played by Diane Keaton, *The Denial of Death* by Ernest Becker (1973, winner of the Pulitzer Prize for General Nonfiction in 1974) and *Death and Western Thought* by Jacques Choron (also 1973). Annie buys a cat book.

28

1912: While Captain Scott makes his doomed attempt at the South Pole, a separate expedition team at Cape Adare, the Northern Party, are forced to overwinter in a snow cave they dig themselves. One of the group, George Murray Levick, describes how they pass the time in

The Illustrated Police News

Law Courts and Weekly Record

ESTABLISHED 1864.

[REGISTERED FOR CIRCULATION IN THE UNITED KINGDOM AND ABROAD.]

SATURDAY, MAY 4, 1895.

Price One Penny.

CLOSING SCENE AT THE OLD BAILEY.

TRIAL OF OSCAR WILDE

OSCAR WILDE AS A LECTURER 1882 AMERICA.

OSCAR WILDE AS A PRISONER 1895 BOW STREET

JURY

SALE OF OSCAR WILDE'S EFFECTS

OSCAR WILDE'S HOUSE 16 TITE STREET.

IMPROVED AND ENLARGED.

some notes he makes on this day: 'I started reading to the party in the evenings. Our library consisted of *David Copperfield*, *Simon the Jester*, the Life of R. L. S. and Boccaccio's *Decameron*. I started on *David Copperfield* and read a chapter every night.'

The Borrowers go up in a balloon in *The Borrowers Aloft* (1959) by Mary Norton, although Arrietty thinks it feels more like mid-April.

29

1952: E. B. White writes to his editor Cass Cranfield about *Charlotte's Web*, unsure of how it will be received. 'Whether children will find anything amusing in it, time will tell.' He wonders if he would have been better off writing about a spaceship heading off towards Mars.

30

1926: Henry Williamson goes to the remote Cranmere Pool on Dartmoor with his brother-in-law Robert to research locations for *Tarka the Otter*. He notes in the visitor book that he 'spurred a big dog [male otter] out of a boggy hollow'. He returns to Cranmere Pool on 17 July 1932 with Charles Tunnicliffe, who is illustrating a new edition of *Tarka*.

31

1988: Toni Morrison wins the Pulitzer Prize for her novel *Beloved*. It follows criticism that she has been overlooked earlier in the year for the National Book and National Book Critics Circle awards.

FINAL WORDS

'The ladder, quickly, bring me the ladder.'
Nikolai Gogol (4 March 1852)

*'Oh, I am not going to die, am I? He will not
separate us. We have been so happy.'*
Charlotte Brontë (31 March 1855)

*'Go on, get out. Last words are for fools
who haven't said enough.'*
Karl Marx (14 March 1883), to his housekeeper

'I'm better now.'
D. H. Lawrence (2 March 1930)

'Everything's gone wrong, my girl.'
Arnold Bennett (27 March 1931) to his mistress Dorothy Cheston

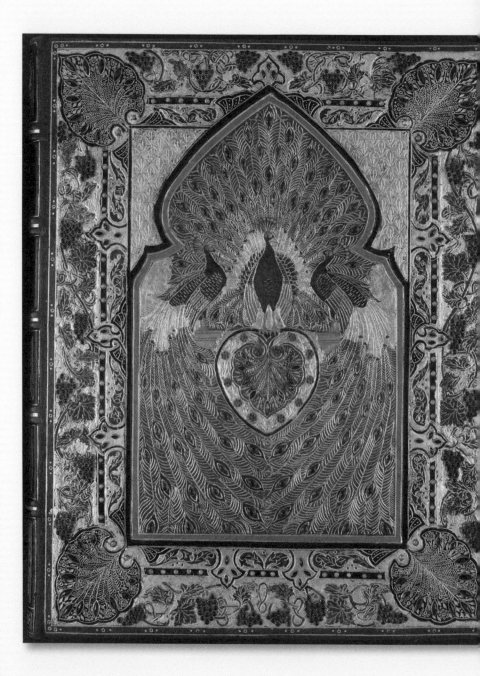

APRIL

'Snow in April is abominable,' said Anne.
'Like a slap in the face when you expected a kiss.'
Anne of Ingleside (1939) by L. M. (Lucy Maud) Montgomery

Births
Milan Kundera (1 April 1929)
Louise Glück (22 April 1943)
Barbara Kingsolver (8 April 1955)
Benjamin Zephaniah (15 April 1958)
Cressida Cowell (15 April 1966)

Deaths
Anna Sewell (25 April 1878)
Dame Muriel Spark (13 April 2006)
Kurt Vonnegut (11 April 2007)
J. G. Ballard (19 April 2009)
Sue Townsend (10 April 2014)

First published/performed
29 April 29 1852: *Roget's Thesaurus* (*Thesaurus of English Words and Phrases Classified and Arranged so as to Facilitate the Expression of Ideas and Assist in Literary Composition* by Peter Roget)
4 April 1860: *The Mill on the Floss* by George Eliot
11 April 1914: *Pygmalion* by George Bernard Shaw
10 April 1925: *The Great Gatsby* by F. Scott Fitzgerald
1 April 2007: *Diary of a Wimpy Kid* by Jeff Kinney

1

1977: Richard Booth, second-hand bookshop owner and the man behind turning Hay-on-Wye into the world's first book town, marches through its streets to the gates of the castle wearing a homemade crown and fake ermine robe. He declares Hay an independent sovereign state and himself 'King Richard I of Hay', also to be known as Richard Cœur de Livre. On the same date twenty-three years later he institutes the Hay House of Lords and creates twenty-one hereditary peers.

2012: The British Library makes a remarkable discovery in one of its holdings, a mid-fourteenth century cookbook by Geoffrey Fule which includes a recipe for unicorns. The book also contains recipes for codswallop and tripe. Two years later, it also notices what appears to be an alien spaceship in the fifteenth-century Huth Hours, confirming contemporary testimony by Lionel the Imbecile.

2

1929: The *Evening News* runs an article on George Bernard Shaw's writing hut, 'The "Little Wooden Hut" of GBS';

'From behind a high hedge … the clicking of a typewriter broke the stillness. It was Mr Bernard Shaw on holiday. Over the barbed wire fence that runs along the bottom of his garden a reporter hailed Mr Shaw and asked him how he was spending Eastertide. "I am not 'spending' Easter," he replied. "I am working it – and working it very hard." He resumed his typing with great vigour. Surrounded by high hedges and cunningly planted clusters of trees and bushes the playwright sat typing in sylvan seclusion in his three-sided revolving "sun trap" hut at the end of his garden.'

The Laurels.

1967: Adrian Mole is 'born'. In his entry for 1981, he notes that he is fourteen and has received a tracksuit and football as presents from his father. For his fortieth birthday he receives a Smythson A4 moleskin notebook from Pandora.

3

Having moved into his new house 'The Laurels', Brickfield Terrace, Holloway ('a nice six-roomed residence, not counting basement, with a front breakfast-parlour'), Mr Pooter makes his first journal entry in *The Diary of a Nobody* (1892) by George and Weedon Grossmith. 'Tradesmen called for custom, and I promised Farmerson, the ironmonger, to give him a turn if I wanted any nails or tools. By-the-by, that reminds me there is no key to our bedroom door, and the bells must be seen to. The parlour bell is broken, and the front door rings up in the servant's bedroom, which is ridiculous. Dear friend Gowing dropped in, but wouldn't stay, saying there was an infernal smell of paint.'

4

Nineteen Eighty-Four, also known as *1984*, by George Orwell begins with Winston Smith starting a diary on this day. This is a dangerous enterprise since while it is not technically illegal, there is the potential for it to be punishable by death or twenty-five years in a forced-labour camp if discovered.

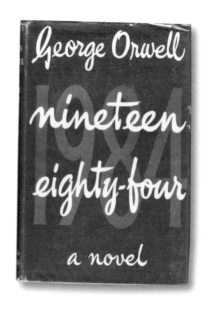

1778: Aged eighty-three, Voltaire (real name François-Marie Arouet) is initiated into Freemasonry, a month before he dies, at la Loge des Neuf Sœurs in Paris. He becomes an Entered Apprentice Freemason.

1968: Distraught at the assassination of her friend Martin Luther King Jr earlier in the day, Maya Angelou goes to a party with James Baldwin on her fortieth birthday at book editor Judy Feiffer's apartment in Manhattan. She fascinates the other guests, including Philip Roth and Feiffer's cartoonist husband, Jules, as she talks about her often appalling childhood experiences publicly for the first time. Feiffer is particularly drawn to Angelou's life story and suggests she writes a memoir – this will become *I Know Why the Caged Bird Sings* (1969).

5

1859: Charles Darwin sends the first three chapters of his *On the Origin of Species* to the publisher John Murray. In his accompanying letter he writes that while Chapter 2 is dull and abstruse, Chapter 3 is plain and interesting. 'It may be conceit, but I believe the subject will interest the public & I am sure that the views are original.' It will be published on 24 November.

6

1327: At mass on Good Friday in the Church of Sainte-Claire d'Avignon, Italian poet Petrarch (Francesco Petrarca) sees Laura. He spends the next decade obssessed with her as she becomes his unwitting muse. Laura's identity is not clear, but she may have been the wife of Count Hugues de Sade.

1626: Essayist, philosopher, scientist and politician, Sir Francis Bacon, is said by seventeenth-century biographer John Aubrey to have been travelling on this day (or possibly the day before) by coach through Highgate, London. Bacon was struck by the idea that snow could perhaps preserve meat, so hopped out, bought a chicken, asked a local woman to disembowel it, and stuffed it with snow. Consequently, Bacon contracted pneumonia and died on 9 April. It's not clear if this story is 100% true, although there have been occasional reported sightings of the chicken as a ghost ...

1958: John Steinbeck writes to his friend and agent Elizabeth Otis that he is planning to build a writer's hut, or what he describes as a 'little lighthouse'. He tells her it will be out of bounds to everybody, and to make sure he plans to install an impressive padlock on the door. He calls his hexagonal garden office 'Joyous Garde' after Sir Lancelot's castle, and deliberately makes it too small to hold a bed so it can never be used as guest accommodation. He will later write *Travels with Charley* (1962) in here.

7

In Nikolai Gogol's short story 'The Nose' (1836), the said organ reappears on this day on the face of Major Kovalyov, having had an exciting time on its own as a State Councillor and narrowly failing to escape from St Petersburg on a coach.

1775: Samuel Johnson pronounces that 'Patriotism is the last refuge of a scoundrel', which is noted by James Boswell, who points out that he means 'pretended patriotism' as a cloak for self-interest rather than 'a real and generous love of our country'.

ENGLISH DICTIONARY

8

1809: Three days earlier Jane Austen writes to publishers Crosby & Co. pointing out that they bought her novel *Susan* six years ago in 1803 and yet it still has not come out, perhaps because somebody has lost the manuscript? On this day, Richard Crosby replies:

'It is true that at the time mentioned we purchased of Mr Seymour a MS novel entitled *Susan* and paid him for it the sum of 10£ for which we have his stamped receipt as a full consideration, but there was not any time stipulated for its publication, neither are we bound to publish it. Should you or anyone else we shall take proceedings to stop the sale. The MS shall be yours for the same as we paid for it.'

1819: After an almost fatal attack of gallstones during the previous month, Sir Walter Scott feels well enough to return to his work in progress, *The Bride of Lammermoor*, which he started six months earlier. But he's not well enough to write, so he dictates the remaining chapters to a secretary.

9

1859: The twenty-three-year-old Samuel Clemens (later to find fame as 'Mark Twain') gets his steamboat pilot's licence after a two-year apprenticeship.

1980: Writer Stephen Spender recalls in his diary that he was at Seattle airport some years previously. Showing his credit card to an airline ticket clerk to prove his identity, he was asked if he was in any way related to the famous poet. Spender replied that he was indeed the famous poet in question. 'Gee,' the impressed clerk replied, 'a near-celebrity.'

10

1710: The Statute of Anne (long title: '*An Act for the Encouragement of Learning, by Vesting the Copies of Printed Books in the Authors or Purchasers of such Copies, during the Times Therein Mentioned*') comes into force in Britain. It is the world's first modern copyright act, with copyright being regulated by the government rather than privately by the Stationers' Company printers' guild, which authors are not allowed to join. Rather than copyright belonging to printers, it now rests with authors for a term of fourteen years, renewable for a further fourteen, before a work then falls into the public domain. Books already in print are granted twenty-one years of protection. Anybody infringing the statute is to receive the stiff fine of a penny for every sheet of the book, proceeds to be split between Crown and author, and have the book destroyed. The act remains in force until the 1842 Copyright Act replaces it.

1816: When Lord Byron meets Samuel Taylor Coleridge on this day (in fact the only time the two poetic giants meet in person), he manages to persuade him to publish his poem 'Kubla Khan' written twenty years earlier (despite the alleged intervention of a 'person on business from Porlock'). Coleridge remarks that Byron is so flattering that is is 'enough to make one's hair bristle' but is also hugely impressed with his lordship, writing in a letter that same day that:

'If you had seen Lord Byron, you could scarcely believe him – so beautiful a countenance I scarcely ever saw – his teeth so many stationary smiles – his eyes the open portals of the sun – things of light and for light – and his forehead so ample, and yet so flexible, passing from marble smoothness into a hundred wreathes and lines and dimples correspondent to the feelings and sentiment he is uttering.'

Poet and essayist Leigh Hunt is also visiting and testifies to the occasion in his own book, *Lord Byron and some of his Contemporaries*:

'He recited his "Kubla Khan" one morning to Lord Byron, in his Lordship's house in Piccadilly, when I happened to be in another room. I remember the other's coming away from him, highly struck with his poem, and saying how wonderfully he talked. This was the impression of everyone who heard him.'

Coleridge signs a contract with publisher John Murray on 12 April and 'Kubla Khan' is published alongside his other works 'Christabel' and 'The Pains of Sleep' on 25 May.

11

1818: Coleridge goes for a two-mile walk in the late evening with John Keats – their only meeting – after they bump into each other near

Kenwood, on the edge of Hampstead Heath. He writes to his brother George that their chat covers many topics, including nightingales, poetry, poetical sensation, metaphysics, types of dreams, consciousness, will and volition, monsters, the Kraken, mermaids and ghost stories. In good humour, Keats describes Coleridge's walking speed as 'alderman-after-dinner pace'. Coleridge remarks that, although Keats seems fit and healthy, when they shake hands goodbye he feels that 'there is death in his hand'. Keats dies three years later, aged twenty-five.

12

1850: 'I have likewise read one of Miss Austen's works *Emma* – read it with interest and with just the degree of admiration which Miss Austen herself would have thought sensible and suitable – anything like warmth or enthusiasm; anything energetic, poignant, heartfelt, is utterly out of place in commending these works: all demonstration the authoress would have met with a well-bred sneer, would have calmly scorned as outré and extravagant … she ruffles her reader by nothing vehement, disturbs him by nothing profound: the Passions are perfectly unknown to her; she rejects even a speaking acquaintance with that stormy Sisterhood …' Charlotte Brontë, letter to W. S. Williams.

13

1992: Our Lady's Choral Society in Dublin begins what will become an annual performance of extracts from George Frederic Handel's oratorio *Messiah*, first performed on this date 250 years previously in Mr Neal's New Musik Hall on Fishamble Street. Now that the hall is demolished, the singers assemble on the same site for 'Messiah on the Street' and over the years expand the offering to include soloists and the Dublin Handelian Orchestra.

2001: *Bridget Jones's Diary*, the film of the 1996 book by Helen Fielding, premieres today, featuring walk-on parts for Jeffrey Archer, Salman Rushdie and Julian Barnes in a book launch scene. Sebastian Faulks, Amanda Foreman and Alain de Botton are also among the guests, but when the scene is reduced in length they do not make it into the final cut.

14–15

1912: On her maiden voyage en route from Southampton to New York, the RMS *Titanic* sinks after colliding with an iceberg. Among the writers who die at sea are American book collector and Grolier Club member Harry Elkins Widener, who at twenty-seven has already amassed an impressive personal library of 2,500 rare books. In a letter from 10 March to a friend, he says he is about to embark on the *Titanic* and has recently bought the complete set of original drawings for *The Mystery of Edwin Drood* from London book dealer Bernard Quaritch. Another of his purchases, this one from J. Pearson and Co., which also goes down with the ship, is 'Heavy News of a Horrible Earthquake which Was in the City of Scarbaria in this Present Year', a small pamphlet about a terrible disaster from 1542.

Leading English journalist and newspaper editor W. T. Stead also dies in the wreck, as does American detective writer Jacques Futrelle. Books lost to the waters include the fabled 'Great Omar', a sumptuous 1911 *Rubaiyat of Omar Khayyam* in a gold-leaf and multi-jewelled binding by Sangorski & Sutcliffe, and a 1598 second edition of Sir Francis Bacon's *Essays* which Widener has just bought in London. Seven parcels of parchment of the Torah owned by Hersh L. Siebald are also among the *Titanic* cargo claimed as lost.

15

1802: William Wordsworth and his sister Dorothy go for a walk at Ullswater in the Lake District, as Dorothy remarks in her *Grasmere Journal*:

'When we were in the woods beyond Gowbarrow park we saw a few daffodils close to the water side. We fancied that the lake had floated the seeds ashore and that the little colony had so sprung up. But as we went along there were more and yet more and at last under the boughs of the trees, we saw that there was a long belt of them along the shore, about the breadth of a country turnpike road. I never saw daffodils so beautiful they grew among the mossy stones about and about them, some rested their heads upon these stones as on a pillow for weariness and the rest tossed and reeled and danced and seemed as if they verily laughed with the wind that blew upon them over the lake, they looked so gay ever glancing ever changing. This wind blew directly over the lake to them. There was here and there a little knot and a few stragglers a few yards higher up but they were so few as not to disturb the simplicity and unity and life of that one busy highway.'

These daffodils inspire William to write his famous poem 'I Wandered Lonely as a Cloud', which begins:

> *I wandered lonely as a cloud*
> *That floats on high o'er vales and hills,*
> *When all at once I saw a crowd,*
> *A host, of golden daffodils;*
> *Beside the lake, beneath the trees,*
> *Fluttering and dancing in the breeze.*

16

1871: Novelist Fyodor Dostoyevsky has spent nearly a decade in thrall to a ruinous compulsive gambling addiction, a period during which he also writes his major work *Crime and Punishment*. On this day, he writes to his wife Anna Dostoyevskaya saying he'll never gamble again. He probably keeps his word.

17

1397: Geoffrey Chaucer probably reads his early road-trip story *The Canterbury Tales* aloud for the first time, at King Richard II's court and in English, rather than French,

which is the court's lingua franca. Exactly 621 years later, the *Daily Telegraph* describes the event as 'the medieval equivalent of a Netflix boxset binge'. Some scholars also regard this as the day on which the travellers set forth, although 16 April and 18 April are also suggested.

18

1916: President of France Raymond Poincaré bestows the title Chevalier of the Legion of Honour, the country's highest honour, on novelist Edith Wharton for her war-relief efforts in France during the First World War. Living in Paris, she has set up self-supporting *ouvroirs* or workrooms for displaced unemployed seamstresses, secretaries, lace and lingerie makers, as well as convalescent homes and a hospital for tuberculosis sufferers, hostels for refugees, and schools for children fleeing occupied Belgium.

1958: A US court rules that, after a thirteen-year detention following his arrest for treason, poet Ezra Pound should not be held any longer at St Elizabeth's Hospital for the criminally insane in Washington, DC.

19

1928: The last volume of the first edition of the *Oxford English Dictionary* is published, forty-four years after the first volume. It covers *Wise* to *Wyzen*. Publication day is celebrated with ceremonial presentations of the completed dictionary to US President Calvin Coolidge and King George V.

20

1919: Thomas Mann resumes work on *The Magic Mountain* after a break of four years.

21

1894: It's opening night for George Bernard Shaw's new play *Arms and the Man* at the Avenue Theatre in London. The audience love it, except for one man who boos. Shaw is reported as commenting: 'I quite agree with you, sir, but what can two do against so many?' The man is thought to be literary agent R. Goulding Bright, hissing because he believes (mistakenly) that Shaw is mocking the British armed forces. Poet W. B. Yeats is in the audience that night and reports Shaw's response slightly less pithily: 'I assure the gentleman in the gallery that he and I are of exactly the same opinion, but what can we do against a whole house who are of the contrary opinion?'

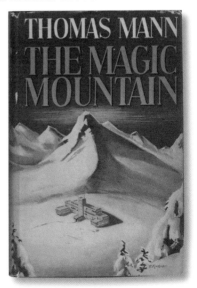

1937: The cartoonist Pont, real name Graham Laidler, starts adding an 'S' discreetly into his cartoons as a secret message to his sweetheart. They are undergoing a six-month separation because her family do not approve of him. By 17 November the 'S' has become a question mark as the couple decide not to pursue their relationship.

22

1884: Cyclist Thomas Stevens starts out from San Francisco on a round-the-world cycling tour on his penny farthing. He is the first person to complete a transcontinental bicycle ride when he reaches Boston on 4 August, and goes on to become the first person to complete the longer route on a bicycle. His book about his adventures becomes the classic *Around the World on a Bicycle (1887).*

1969: At the inaugural Booker Prize ceremony at Stationers' Hall, London, winner P. H. Newby (for *Something to Answer For*) receives a silver-coloured trophy designed by writer and artist Jan Pieńkowski. Apparently inspired by an art deco lamp spotted in London's Portobello Market, it depicts a woman in a pleated sleeveless gown, head turned to the right, hair in a bob, her arms fully extended upwards as she carries a large bowl. It is exactly the same height as the FA Cup.

23

1943: Alison Uttley, best known for her Sam Pig and Little Grey Rabbit series of books, bumps into Enid Blyton in a fishmonger's in Beaconsfield where they both live. Uttley writes that she fails to recognise the famous children's writer, who she says is 'ogling' the fishmonger (although she does note 'her false teeth, her red lips'), until the fishmonger introduces them. She elaborates on this story later in her diaries: when she asks her what kind of books she writes, Blyton tells her to 'Look in Smith's window'.

1975: Novelist Barbara Pym and poet-librarian Philip Larkin meet in person for the first time in the bar of the Randolph Hotel, Oxford, having written letters to each other for the previous fourteen years. Pym tells him that she will be wearing a beige tweed suit or, if it's

Thomas Stevens

Kelly .87

nippy, a Welsh tweed cape. Larkin replies that he is bald, tall, wears glasses and is deaf, but has no idea what he will be wearing. They have lunch by the window looking towards the Ashmolean Musuem.

In Catalonia, today is *la Diada de Sant Jordi* (Saint George's Day), which celebrates the region's patron saint. There was a long-standing tradition that men gave their sweethearts roses on this day, with women reciprocating with a book; now the book swapping has become mutual, making this the region's major book-buying event of the year. In 1995, UNESCO turns it into an international event by naming it World Book Day.

24

Sherlock Holmes protects himself from air-gun fire and reveals the existence of Professor Moriarty to Dr Watson in 'The Final Problem':

'It was with some surprise, therefore, that I saw him walk into my consulting-room upon the evening of April 24th. It struck me that he was looking even paler and thinner than usual.

" HE TURNED HIS ROUNDED BACK UPON ME."

"Yes, I have been using myself up rather too freely," he remarked, in answer to my look rather than to my words; "I have been a little pressed of late. Have you any objection to my closing your shutters?"

The only light in the room came from the lamp upon the table at which I had been reading. Holmes edged his way round the wall and flinging the shutters together, he bolted them securely.

"You are afraid of something?" I asked.

"Well, I am.'"

25

1898: William Sydney Porter, better known in the literary world as writer O. Henry, the author of the much-anthologised and adapted Christmas short story 'The Gift of the Magi', starts a five-year jail sentence for embezzlement (see 24 July).

26

1336: Italian poet Petrarch climbs 1,912 m to the top of Mont Ventoux in Provence, carrying with him a small copy of St Augustine's *Confessions*. He claims he is the first person since antiquity to climb a mountain for pleasure and the view, ignoring an elderly shepherd along the way who says he has already wandered up to the summit and it isn't worth the bother. After problems choosing a suitable walking companion, he settles on his brother, who goes straight up while Petrarch zigzags to deal with the steep inclines. He spends some time at the summit looking back on the mistakes of his past life and resolves to do better in the future.

27

1667: John Milton, blind and in dire financial straits, signs a contract with printer Samuel Simmons in London to publish *Paradise Lost* (in fact it is probably signed on Milton's behalf by his amanuensis and then Milton adds his seal to it). It is the earliest extant example of a contract between a publisher and an English author and is held by the British Library. The advance is £5, with £5 more once 1,300 copies are sold, and £10 promised for a second edition if it sells well. Milton lives long enough to receive the first tenner, but dies before he can collect the second, although his widow Elizabeth is paid £8 on 21 December 1680 for sales up to that point.

28

1962: Police raid the flat of Joe Orton and his lover Kenneth Halliwell, arrest the couple and charge them with stealing seventy-two books and removing 1,653 plates from art books. They have also been defacing the covers of books in Islington Public Library since January 1959, adding inappropriate images to the covers. They receive a six-month prison sentence for theft and malicious damage and are fined £262.

29

1915: After a public competition asking for suggestions, NASA announces the new crater on Mercury will be called after poet, politician and priestess Enheduanna, the world's first named author, a resident of ancient Mesopotamia around the twenty-third century BC and daughter of Sargon the Great.

30

1642: Poet Richard Lovelace is imprisoned for his pro-royalist views. While jailed in Gatehouse Prison next to Westminster Abbey, he probably writes 'To Althea, from Prison', which contains the lines 'Stone walls do not a prison make / Nor iron bars a cage.' The poem endures and is name-checked in *Marchmont* (1796) by Charlotte Smith, *Villette* (1853) by Charlotte Brontë and *Hag-Seed* (2016) by Margaret Atwood, as well as being set to music by Fairport Convention on their 1973 album *Nine*.

FINAL WORDS

'No, it is not'
Oliver Goldsmith (4 April 1774),
when asked if his mind is at ease

'Come, come, no weakness! Let's be a man
to the last' or *'Now, I shall go to sleep. Good night'*
Lord Byron (19 April 1824)

'Give me my glasses' or *'If we meet …'*
Mark Twain (21 April 1910), although a note by his deathbed reads:
'Death, the only immortal, who treats us alike, whose
peace and refuge are for all. The soiled and the pure,
the rich and the poor; the loved and the unloved.'

'Indeed, very good.
I shall have to repeat that on the Golden Floor'
A. E. Housman (30 April 1936), to his doctor
who has just told him a joke.

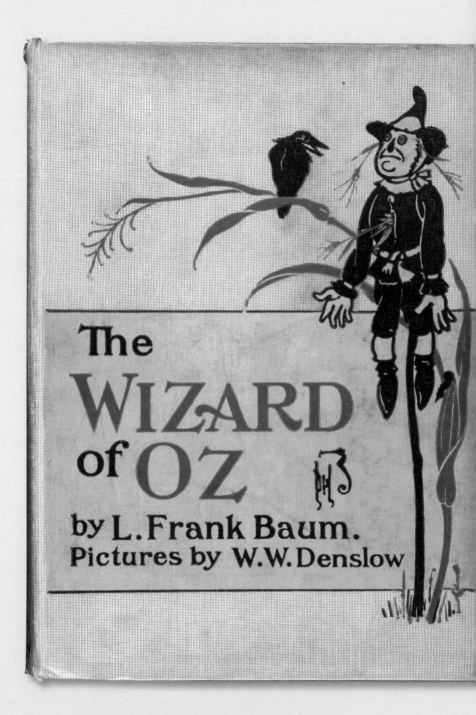

The
WIZARD
of OZ

by L. Frank Baum.
Pictures by W.W. Denslow

MAY

Hail bounteous May that dost inspire
Mirth and youth, and warm desire,
Woods and Groves, are of thy dressing,
Hill and Dale, doth boast thy blessing.
'Song on May Morning' (1645) by John Milton

Births
Margery Allingham (20 May 1904)
Rachel Carson (27 May 1907)
J. L. Carr (20 May 1912)
Angela Carter (7 May 1940)
Simon Armitage (26 May 1963)

Deaths
Gustave Flaubert (8 May 1880)
Emily Dickinson (15 May 1886)
Edward Lear (12 May 1888)
Maurice Sendak (8 May 2012)
Ruth Rendell (2 May 2015)

First published/performed
17 May 1900: *The Wonderful Wizard of Oz* by L Frank Baum
1 May 1901: *The Life of the Bee* by Maurice Maeterlinck
4 May 1925: *Mrs Dalloway* by Virginia Woolf
4 May 1948: *The Naked and the Dead* by Norman Mailer
22 May 2014: *Beowulf*, translated by J. R. R. Tolkien.

THE SPERMACETI WHALE
Beale

1

1850: Herman Melville is getting on well with *Moby-Dick*, as he explains to his friend the lawyer and memoirist Richard Henry Dana Jr in a letter:

'I am half way in the work … It will be a strange sort of book, tho', I fear; blubber is blubber you know; tho' you might get oil out of it, the poetry runs as hard as sap from a frozen maple tree; – and to cool the thing up, one must needs throw in a little fancy, which from the nature of the thing, must be ungainly as the gambols of the whales themselves. Yet I mean to give the truth of the thing, spite of this.'

It is the earliest known mention of the novel.

1954: Aged thirty-six, novelist Muriel Spark is received into the Roman Catholic Church by Maltese priest Dom Ambrose Agius, a year after being baptised in the Church of England. She admits there is no 'blinding revelation' but that as a result she begins 'to see life as a whole rather than as a series of disconnected happenings' which helps her write her first novel, *The Comforters* (1957).

2009: Carol Ann Duffy is appointed poet laureate of the United Kingdom. She is the first woman, the first Scot and the first openly gay person to hold the position.

2

1936: Edna St Vincent Millay takes her only manuscript copy of her work in progress, *Conversations at Midnight*, with her on holiday to Sanibel Island, Florida. She checks in to the Sanibel Palms Hotel, has her luggage sent up to her room and then goes for a stroll on the nearby beach. When she turns around, the hotel is on fire and her sequence of poems goes up in flames with it, along with her seventeenth-century edition of poems by Catullus. She starts again from scratch and the book is published the following year.

3

2020: Bernardine Evaristo becomes the latest celebrity to sit for Sky Arts' lockdown portrait series *Portrait Artist of the Week*, hosted by Joan Bakewell. It is a version of the channel's show *Portrait Artist of the Year* and features famous people sitting at home allowing artists in their own homes to produce portraits of them and send them in for judging. Evaristo sits for four hours as previous series winner Duncan Shoosmith paints her live via a Facebook feed.

1810: The twenty-two-year-old Lord Byron swims the Hellespont, the strait in Turkey better known today as the Dardanelles which separates Europe from Asia. He takes on the four-mile challenge as a tribute to Leander, who in Greek mythology swam the divide every night to visit his lover, Hero. Byron claims it takes him an hour and ten minutes, writing to his publisher John Murray the following year: 'The *tide* was *not* in our favour; on the contrary, the great difficulty was to bear up against the current … My own experience and that of others

bids me pronounce the passage of Leander perfectly practicable. Any young man, in good and tolerable skill in swimming, might succeed in it from *either* side.'

Travel writer Patrick Leigh Fermor also manages it in 1984 aged sixty-nine (swimming at a pace reminiscent, he says, of a 'Victorian clergyman'). It takes him three hours. To celebrate the bicentenary of Byron's swim, 140 swimmers follow in his wavesteps, with 120 finishing successfully.

4

1699: In *Gulliver's Travels*, Lemuel Gulliver begins his journey.

'We set sail from Bristol, May 4, 1699, and our voyage was at first very prosperous. It would not be proper, for some reasons, to trouble the reader with the particulars of our adventures in those seas; let it suffice to inform him, that in our passage from thence to the East Indies, we were driven by a violent storm to the north-west of Van Diemen's Land. By an observation, we found ourselves in the latitude of 30 degrees 2 minutes south.'

1891: Sherlock Holmes appears to die at the Reichenbach Falls in Switzerland in Arthur Conan Doyle's short story 'The Final Problem'. Conan Doyle sets the story in the immediate past, having visited the falls in 1893 and noting in his diary that he wants to kill Holmes there.

5

1893: Jonathan Harker meets the infamous count at his castle in the Carpathian Mountains in Bram Stoker's *Dracula*.

1926: American writer Sinclair Lewis refuses the Pulitzer Prize for his novel *Arrowsmith,* saying: 'All prizes, like all titles, are dangerous. The seekers for prizes tend to labor not for inherent excellence but for alien rewards: they tend to write this, or timorously to avoid writing that, in order to tickle the prejudices of a haphazard committee. And the Pulitzer Prize for novels is peculiarly objectionable because the terms of it have been constantly and grievously misrepresented.'

6

Dorigen makes her seemingly watertight promise to Arveragus (that she will transfer her love from her husband to him if he removes all the rocks from the coast of Brittany) in Geoffrey Chaucer's 'Franklin's Tale' from *The Canterbury Tales* (*c*. 1397).

So on a day, right in the morwe-tyde,
Unto a gardyn that was ther bisyde,

In which that they hadde maad hir ordinaunce
Of vitaille and of oother purveiaunce,
They goon and pleye hem al the longe day.
And this was on the sixte morwe of May,
Which May hadde peynted with his softe shoures
This gardyn ful of leves and of floures

7

1932: Aged thirty-four, at the top of his game literarily but wobbly financially, novelist William Faulkner arrives in Hollywood to begin working as a screenwriter for MGM. In fact he arrives drunk, strangely unkempt and bleeding from a cut on his head from an incident of mysterious origin. Unable to get to grips with the studio system (he has an idea about a Mickey Mouse film, not realising that the character is a Disney rather than MGM property), he disappears entirely for seven days and ends up wandering around Death Valley, some 150 miles away.

8

Year of the 58th Hunger Games: Katniss Everdeen is born in District 12 (according to the film, since the date is not mentioned in the book).

9

1662: During a busy day, Samuel Pepys makes time 'to see an Italian puppet play that is within the rayles there, which is very pretty, the best that ever I saw, and great resort of gallants'. It is the first recorded mention of Mr Punch in England, performed by Pietro Gimonde using marionettes rather than hand puppets. The site of this first performance is commemorated in a plaque. Pepys obviously likes the show because he goes to another, probably performed by puppeteer Anthony Devoto, on 10 November.

1869: Henry James and George Eliot meet for the first time, as James explains in a letter written to his father the next day:

'I was immensely impressed, interested & pleased. To begin with she is magnificently ugly – deliciously hideous. She has a low forehead, a dull grey eye, a vast pendulous nose, a huge mouth, full of uneven teeth & a chin & jawbone *qui n'en finissent pas* … Now in this vast ugliness resides a most powerful beauty which, in a very few minutes steals forth & charms the mind, so that you end as I ended, in falling in love with her. Yes behold me literally in love with this great horse-faced blue-stocking. I don't know in what the charm lies, but it is thoroughly potent. An admirable physiognomy – a delightful expression, a voice soft & rich as that of a counselling angel – a mingled sagacity & sweetness – a broad hint of a great underlying world of reserve, knowledge, pride & power – a great feminine dignity & character in these massively plain features – a hundred conflicting shades of consciousness & simpleness – shyness & frankness – graciousness & remote indifference – these are some of the more definite elements of her personality. Her manner is extremely good tho' rather too intense & her speech, in the way of accent & syntax peculiarly agreeable. Altogether, she has a larger circumference than any woman I have ever seen.'

10

1849: The escalating nationalistic rivalry between two Shakespearean actors, the Englishman William Macready (see 16 August) and the American Edwin Forrest, reaches fever pitch when a riot breaks out at the Astor Opera House, Manhattan, as Macready performs his Macbeth. Heavy-handed policing of the angry mob of thousands outside the theatre results in at least two dozen deaths and around 250 injured, including many policemen.

1907: While on holiday in Cornwall, Kenneth Grahame writes a letter to his son Alastair, who has remained at home with his nanny. 'Have you heard about the Toad?' he asks. It is the first of more than a

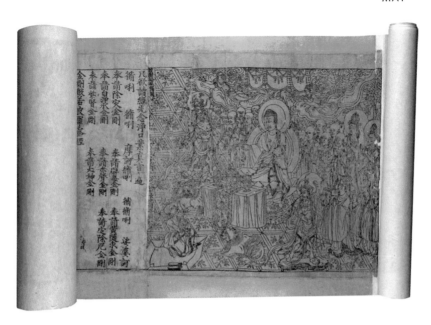

dozen letters over the next couple of months which include the tale of the now familiar characters as a replacement for Alastair's usual bedtime story. That first missive – held today by the Bodleian Library in Oxford – is also a birthday letter for Alastair, and Grahame adds that he has sent him a Brer Rabbit book as a present, as well as a toy boat, some sand toys and a card game.

11

868: The Diamond Sutra, now in the British Library, is published in China. It is the earliest dated example of woodblock printing, as well as the earliest surviving dated complete printed book.

12

1963: The 1987 film *Dirty Dancing* premieres in Cannes, France. In an early scene, medical student Robbie, working as a waiter, tries to give Baby his much-read copy of Ayn Rand's *The Fountainhead*. 'Read it,' he says. 'I think you'll enjoy it, but return it. I have notes in there.' Baby does not take it.

13

Julian of Norwich's Catholic feast day (it's 8 May in the Anglican church) is the day the mystic recovered from her near-fatal illness, during which she received visions of Christ. Her devotional writings, now known as *Revelations of Divine Love*, are the earliest surviving English-language works by a woman, and the only surviving ones by an anchoress.

1703: Samuel Pepys adds a second codicil to his will with instructions for what should happen to his impressive personal library of 3,000 volumes (and that of his nephew, John Jackson) after his death to make sure it is not broken up. It should go to a university, preferably Cambridge not Oxford, preferably Magdalene College not Trinity; it should have its own room; its books should not leave the library; and nobody can take out more than ten at once.

14

1899: In *The Hound of the Baskervilles* by Arthur Conan Doyle, the *Devon County Chronicle* runs a story about the death of Sir Charles Baskerville, concluding he has died of heart failure, and failing to mention any frighteningly large canine.

1912: Edgar Rice Burroughs finishes writing *Tarzan of the Apes* at 10.25 p.m., having started it at 8 p.m. on 1 December 1911.

15

1870: While philosopher Friedrich Engels is living in Manchester in the 1840s, he and Karl Marx regularly meet up, especially in 1845, when the two theorists study together in the Reading Room at the city's Chetham's Library, the oldest free public library in Britain. On this date, Engels writes nostalgically to Marx: 'In the last few days I have often been sitting at the quadrilateral desk in the small bow-window where we sat 24 years ago; I like this place very much; because of its coloured window the weather is always fine there. Old Jones the librarian is still around, but he is very old and does nothing more; I haven't yet seen him there again.'

16

1763: After trying for some time, James Boswell finally meets Samuel Johnson for the first time at a bookshop owned by Thomas Davies in Covent Garden, London:

'When I was sitting in Mr Davies's back parlour, after having drunk tea with him and Mrs Davies, Johnson unexpectedly came into the shop; and Mr Davies having perceived him through the glass-door in the room in which we were sitting, advancing towards us, – he announced his awful approach to me, somewhat in the manner of an actor in the part of Horatio, when he addresses Hamlet on the appearance of his father's ghost, "Look, my lord, it comes."'

The meeting is a mitigated success. Johnson delivers a mild anti-Scottish insult on discovering Boswell is from north of the border, and Boswell puts his foot in it commenting on Johnson's long friendship with the actor David Garrick. But once Johnson leaves, Davies says to a slightly disconsolate Boswell: 'Don't be uneasy. I can see he likes you very well.'

1904: In the prestigious Feis Ceoil singing competition in Dublin, the young James Joyce sings 'No Chastening' from the oratorio *The Prodigal Son by* Arthur Sullivan, and a traditional Irish song, 'A Long Farewell'. But when the gold medal for tenor solo appears to be his to lose, he flounces off the stage when asked to sight-read a third song, which he is unable to do. In the end Joyce comes third, winning a bronze medal made by Dublin jeweller Edmond Johnson. An urban legend grows up that, disgusted with the result, he throws the medal into the city's Liffey River, but in fact it is bought at Sotheby's years later by dancer and Riverdance choreographer Michael Flatley for £14,400.

1963: Anthony Burgess mischievously reviews a copy of his own new book *Inside Mr Enderby* (written under his pen name Joseph Kell) for his regular fortnightly slot in the *Yorkshire Post*, whose books editor Kenneth Young is not aware that they are the same person. Burgess gives it a fairly negative review, writing that 'those of my readers with tender stomachs are advised to let it alone', but praises 'Enderby's gross richness'. When he finds out though, Young is not amused – Burgess loses the column and an apology appears in the paper regretting what was not a 'disinterested appreciation of the novel'.

17

1824: Lord Byron's memoirs, diaries and correspondence written between 1818 and 1821 are lost for ever when the manuscript is burnt at the office of his publishers, John Murray, in Albemarle Street, London. Murray and five of Byron's friends take the decision because the two volumes are so scandalous. Copies of the 120,000-word work have been sent to various friends including Washington Irving, Lady Caroline Lamb and Percy Shelley, and its general reception is that it is not really all that hot stuff. However, no trace of what they contain survives, despite Byron's nod to posterity that 'When you read my *Memoirs* you will learn the evils, moral and physical, of true dissipation. I can assure you my life is very entertaining and very instructive.'

1928: Evelyn Waugh writes to *The Times* to complain that he was called Miss Waugh throughout its review of his first book, *Rossetti: His Life and Works*, written by poet Sturge Moore seven days earlier ('Miss Waugh approaches the "squalid" Rossetti like some dainty Miss of the sixties'). Waugh conspicuously signs the letter with his full name, Evelyn Arthur St John Waugh.

18

1922: There's an extraordinary guest list for dinner tonight at the Hotel Majestic in Paris, hosted by novelist and literary patron Sydney Schiff. Among the guests are Marcel Proust, James Joyce, Clive Bell from the Bloomsbury set, composers Igor Stravinsky and Erik Satie, Pablo Picasso and ballet mogul Sergei Diaghilev. The dinner is essentially an 'after party' following the premiere earlier in the evening at the Opéra Garnier of Stravinsky's *Renard*, performed by Diaghilev's Ballets Russes.

Dubbed 'the modernist dinner party of the century', it's actually rather a strange and long occasion. Underdressed for the smart evening, Joyce rolls in after midnight somewhat inebriated (or as Clive Bell puts it, 'a good deal the worse for wear'), sits down, continues drinking and barely speaks, before falling asleep. Proust turns up a couple of hours later, dressed all in black with white kid gloves (Stravinsky describes him 'as pale as a mid-afternoon moon'). Proust and Joyce admit they've not read each other's work but bond over their respective medical ailments.

19

1952: Screenwriter and playwright Lillian Hellman refuses to name names at the House Committee on Un-American Activities. She pleads the fifth amendment and goes on the blacklist. Although her career is not completely ruined it is badly damaged as a result.

20

1845: Elizabeth Barrett and Robert Browning meet for the first time at her home in Wimpole Street, London, at 3 p.m. (Browning leaves an hour and a half later). She has already put off the encounter several times – in a letter to her brother George on 30 March 1842, she writes: 'Mr Kenyon proposed also to introduce to my sofa-side … Mr Browning the poet … who was so honor-giving as to wish something of the sort! I was pleased at the thought of his wishing it.'

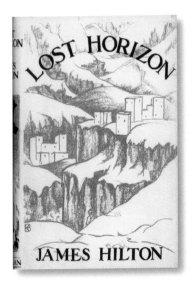

1931: Visionary diplomat Hugh Conway leaves Baskul, Afghanistan, in *Lost Horizon* by James Hilton. He is unwittingly heading towards Shangri-La with a mysterious group of people. He is last seen the following year on 3 February in Bangkok, attempting to get back to the lamasery...

2015: The Office of the Director of National Intelligence begins the first phase of its release of books and documents recovered from the compound hiding Osama bin Laden before his death at the hands of US special operations forces. Among the English-language titles are *Imperial Hubris* by Michael Scheuer; *Handbook of International Law* by Anthony Aust; *Necessary Illusions: Thought Control in Democratic Societies* by Noam Chomsky; *Bloodlines of the Illuminati* by Fritz Springmeier; and *Christianity and Islam in Spain* 756–1031 AD by C. R. Haines.

2016: Numerous writers put their signature to an open letter from British people working in creative industries encouraging voters not to vote for Brexit. Among them are Michael Morpurgo, Philip Pullman, Kate Mosse, poet laureate Carol Ann Duffy, Dame Hilary Mantel, Ian McEwan, John Le Carré, Sir Tom Stoppard, Geoff Dyer, Sally Wainwright, Michael Frayn and Kathy Lette.

21

1944: After three years of bedtime stories about Pippi Långstrump (Pippi Longstocking), Astrid Lindgren presents her daughter Karin with a handwritten book of her adventures for her tenth birthday. She then sends them to publishing firm Bonnier who, after some consideration, reject the book. It is published at Christmas 1945 after Lindgren wins first prize in a children's book competition run by publisher Raben & Sjogren.

22

1961: On the BBC Home Service, Kenneth Williams picks the collected works of George Bernard Shaw as his book on *Desert Island Discs*. He is asked to shipwreck himself again on 31 July 1987, when he picks the classic English poetry anthology *Palgrave's Golden Treasury*, first published in 1861.

23

1895 and 1911: On the first date, the New York Public Library is established, essentially a combination of the city's Astor and Lenox libraries, which are in financial difficulties, together with a major bequest from former Governor Samuel J. Tilden, whose will leaves most of his $2.4 million fortune to help 'establish and maintain a free library and reading room in the city of New York'. On the second date, the new library of more than a million volumes is dedicated

at a special ceremony attended by President William Taft, Governor John Dix and Mayor William Gaynor. The following day, around 40,000 members of the public swarm into the building for the first time.

24

1932: The thirty-one-year-old artist Charles F. Tunnicliffe arrives at Henry Williamson's home in Shallowford to discuss how he will illustrate the forthcoming new edition of *Tarka the Otter* and see the area where it was set. He sends his first-draft efforts for approval on 8 June, then returns on 15 July to look more closely at Canal Bridge, where Tarka is born and dies. On 17 July he walks up to Cranmere Pool with Williamson. By 12 August Tunnicliffe has finished.

25

1911: Thomas Mann visits Venice with his wife Katia and his brother Heinrich and is inspired to write his novella *Death in Venice*, not least by his observation of young Polish boy, Władysław Moes, who is the basis for Tadzio. Indeed, in his 1930 book *A Sketch of My Life*, Mann admits that 'Nothing in *Death in Venice* is invented', including the mysterious gondolier, the luggage mix-up, the cholera, the travel agent and the street singer. He stays until 2 June.

2001: Fans of Douglas Adams – who died a fortnight previously – celebrate the first Towel Day, an event that subsequently becomes an annual occasion on which people carry towels as a mark of respect. A towel, as *The Hitchhiker's Guide to the Galaxy* explains, is 'about the most massively useful thing an interstellar hitchhiker can have'.

1992: The Rock Bottom Remainders play their first concert at the annual American Library Association conference in Anaheim, California. Made up of writers who are also musicians, the revolving personnel who play over the next two decades include Stephen King (on rhythm guitar), Amy Tan, Dave Barry (on lead guitar), Scott Turow and Barbara Kingsolver (on keyboards), with Maya Angelou as an honorary member. The group plays its final concert, again at the American Library Association conference in Anaheim, on 23 June 2012, having raised more than $2 million over the previous two decades for charity. In the foreword to his book *On Writing* (2000), King describes the band as 'pretty good. You'd pay to hear us.'

26

2012: The first World Dracula Day is organised by the Whitby Dracula Society 1897 (Bram Stoker's *Dracula* was first published in 1897). In 2022, 1,369 people dress as vampires and assemble at Whitby

Abbey, the inspiration for Stoker's story. They successfully break the world record for the largest crowd of vampires, all participants adhering to a strict dress code of:

black trousers/dress
black shoes
waistcoat
shirt
black cape/collared overcoat
fangs

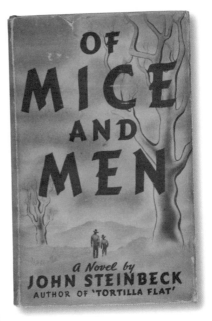

27

1936: John Steinbeck's dog Toby eats most of the first draft of *Of Mice and Men*. Steinbeck describes it as a 'minor tragedy' and it sets him back two months in the book's writing. In a letter to his editor, Elizabeth Otis, he adds that he has made the Irish setter pup 'lieutenant-colonel in charge of literature'.

28

1988: The first Hay Festival opens in Welsh book town Hay-on-Wye and runs until 31 May.

29

1550: The boy king Edward VI's diary is now held by the British Library. Here is a typical entry: 'The embassadours had a fair souper made them by the duke of Somerset, and afterward went into the tems [on the Thames] and saw both the beare hunted in the river, and also wilfier cast out of botis, and many pretty conceites.'

30

1593: Playwright Christopher Marlowe dies, according to official contemporary reports, after being stabbed by businessman Ingram Frizer over a financial dispute in Deptford, London. However, many more conspiracy theories have since been put forward, from privy councillors going rogue to Marlowe faking his death and going on to write Shakespeare's plays.

1669: Samuel Pepys writes his final diary entry after nearly ten years of keeping his journal.

31

1897: After several days of rumours circulating that Mark Twain has died in London, he writes a letter, often misquoted, to the *New York Journal*'s London editor, Frank Marshall White. 'I can understand perfectly how the report of my illness got about, I have even heard on good authority that I was dead. James Ross Clemens, a cousin of mine, was seriously ill two or three weeks ago in London, but is well now. The report of my illness grew out of his illness. The report of my death was an exaggeration.' An article confirming this appears in the *Journal* on 2 June.

FINAL WORDS

'Here I am, dying of a hundred good symptoms.'
Alexander Pope (30 May 1744), to his doctor
remarking on his patient's positive condition

'Here is the battle of day against night. I see black light.'
Victor Hugo (22 May 1885)

'I must go in. The fog is rising.'
Emily Dickinson (15 May 1886)

'On the contrary.'
Henrik Ibsen (23 May 1906), replying to his maid
who claims he is getting healthier

'Now we can cross the shifting sands'
L. Frank Baum (5 May 1919)

LES
FLEURS DU MAL

AMBROISE VOLLARD, ÉDITEUR

6, Rue Laffitte, 6

IMPRIMERIE NATIONALE

PARIS

1916

JUNE

Yes, I remember Adlestrop –
The name, because one afternoon
Of heat the express-train drew up there
Unwontedly. It was late June.
'Adlestrop' (1917) by Edward Thomas (see 24 June)

Births
Catherine Cookson (27 June 1906)
Anthony Buckeridge (20 June 1912)
Laurie Lee (26 June 1914)
Vikram Seth (20 June 1952)
Val McDermid (4 June 1955)

Deaths
Charles Dickens (9 June 1870)
Tove Jansson (27 June 2001)
José Saramago (18 June 2010)
Tom Sharpe (6 June 2013)
Michael Bond (27 June 2017)

First published/performed
25 June 1857: *Les Fleurs du mal* by Charles Baudelaire
20 June 1903: *The Call of the Wild* by Jack London
4 June 1924: *A Passage to India* by E. M. Forster
25 June 1947: *Het Achterhuis* (*The Diary of a Young Girl*) by Anne Frank
26 June 1997: *Harry Potter and the Philosopher's Stone* by J. K. Rowling

1

1885: Although he requests a poor man's send-off with no formal religious service, an estimated two million people turn out in Paris for the state funeral procession of novelist and statesman Victor Hugo. Some people have been gathering for several days before and there is a remarkable party atmosphere on the big day, with restaurants, brothels and shops shutting. The procession runs from the Arc de Triomphe up to the Panthéon where he is buried, a final resting place now shared with fellow writers Alexandre Dumas and Émile Zola.

2

1853: 'The praise you accord to my "budding" English, I find most encouraging. What I chiefly lack is first, assurance as to grammar and secondly, skill in using various secondary idioms which alone enable

one to write with any pungency.' Karl Marx, letter written in Dean Street, Soho, to Friedrich Engels in Manchester.

3

1952: At 1.34 a.m., Tintin and his fellow astronauts Captain Haddock, Professor Calculus, Frank Wolff and Snowy the dog are launched into space as their rocket heads to the moon in *Destination Moon* (*Objectif Lune* in the original French, first published in book form 1953).

4

1831: Elizabeth Barrett Browning, aged twenty-five, starts a diary:

'I wonder if I shall burn this sheet of paper like most others I have begun in the same way. To write a diary, I have thought of very often at far & near distances of time: but how could I write a diary without throwing upon paper my thoughts, all my thoughts – the thoughts of my heart as well as of my head? – and then how could I bear to look on them after they were written? Adam made fig leaves necessary for the mind, as well as for the body. And such a mind I have! So very exacting & exclusive & eager & headlong – & strong & so very very often wrong! Well! But I will write: I must write – & the oftener wrong I know myself to be, the less wrong I shall be in one thing – the less vain I shall be!'

5

1934: The Baker Street Irregulars Society holds its first dinner in New York City, thus becoming the first Sherlockian society. It beats the English Sherlock Society, which holds its first dinner on 7 June, by two days. Initially membership is men only, and the first woman member is Arthur Conan Doyle's daughter and literary executor, Dame Jean Conan Doyle, in 1991. Famous members over the years include Isaac Asimov, Neil Gaiman, Sherlock/Conan Doyle expert Richard Lancelyn Green, Rex Stout, Edith Meiser, and Nicholas Meyer, author of the novel *The Seven-Per-Cent Solution*.

1944: At 9.15 p.m., the BBC's Radio Londres broadcasts three lines from Paul Verlaine's poem 'Chanson d'automne' (1866):

Blessent mon coeur
D'une langueur
Monotone.

It is a message from Allied forces to a resistance unit south of Orléans telling it to start sabotaging railway lines as part of the imminent D Day offensive in Normandy. German forces intercept it, realise it means something important, but cannot work out exactly what is being planned. The event inspires the establishment of the Verlaine Message Museum, or Museum of 5 June 1944.

6

1928: Prime Minister Stanley Baldwin gives a humorous and congratulatory speech at a nine-course banquet at the Worshipful Company of Goldsmiths in London to celebrate the completion of the *Oxford English Dictionary*. It is, he says, 'unrivalled in completeness and unapproachable in authority, as near infallibility, indeed, as we can hope to get this side of Rome'. The 100 guests enjoy caviar, smoked salmon and lobster, washed down with half a dozen wines including an 1896 Crofts and a 1907 Chateau Margaux. No women are invited, not even Rosfrith Murray, who has worked on the dictionary for twenty years.

1944: Sergeant J. D. Salinger, alongside his fellow Fourth Infantry Division soldiers, lands on Utah Beach on D Day with six draft chapters of *The Catcher in the Rye* in his pockets. He is part of the second wave. Later that year, after the invasion of Normandy, Salinger goes on to take part in the Battle of the Bulge and the Battle of Hürtgen Forest, meeting Ernest Hemingway for the first and only time at the Hotel Ritz after the liberation of Paris. They get on really well.

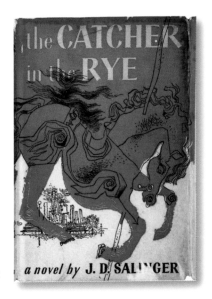

1964: After a friendly correspondence during which T. S. Eliot asks Groucho Marx for a photo of the comedian, the author of *The Waste Land* and the screen star who played Rufus T. Firefly in *Duck Soup* meet for dinner in London. In a letter of 3 June, Eliot thanks Groucho for telling the newspapers he has come to London largely to see Eliot, adding that it has improved his street credibility among neighbours, especially his greengrocer. Eliot arranges for a car to pick up Groucho and his wife Eden and bring them to his home, and then take the couple home again after dinner, during which Groucho quotes part of *The Waste Land* back to its creator.

7

1912: 'Bad. Wrote nothing today.' Franz Kafka, diary entry.

1944: Five years to the day after he meets his second wife, the editor and writer Margerie Bonner, the fourth draft of *Under the Volcano* is nearly lost when Malcolm Lowry's wooden beach cabin in Dollarton, British Columbia, burns to the ground. All his work in progress is lost, although Margerie manages to rescue the manuscript – while he saves Margerie's latest story, 'The Shapes That Creep' – and on 6 June the following year Lowry submits it to a literary agent in New York. Lowry's 1,000-page unpublished novel *In Ballast to the White Sea* is long thought to have been lost in the flames too, but happily a copy has been made and an edition is published in 2014.

8

793: According to the *Anglo-Saxon Chronicle* entry for this year, Viking warriors plunder the monastery at Lindisfarne. Miraculously, amid the destruction the illuminated early eighth-century Lindisfarne Gospels survive undamaged. When the monks leave in *c.* 875, they take the precious book with them.

9

1941: As the Nabokov family enjoy a motoring holiday in America, they stop for a few days at the Grand Canyon's southern rim. Up early on this morning, with his freshly issued permit to collect butterflies in hand, keen lepidopterist Vladimir sets off along Bright Angel Trail with Dorothy Leuthold, one of his students, who is helping out with the driving. When Dorothy accidentally nearly treads on a brown butterfly, Nabokov recognises it as an unknown species, catches it, and names it after Leuthold. *Neonympha dorothea* comes to be known as 'canyonland satyr' or 'Dorothy's satyr'. A few days later Nabokov writes a poem about the experience, 'On Discovering a Butterfly', in which he describes how he became 'godfather to an insect and its first describer – and I want no other fame'.

10

1881: Looking for meaning in life after finding literary success with *War and Peace* and *Anna Karenina*, the fifty-two-year-old Leo Tolstoy sets off on pilgrimage to the Optina Pustyn monastery. Dressed as a peasant and wearing shoes made of bark, he gets blisters on the way and takes the train home.

1930: Sentenced to death by Mr Justice Lawrence Wargrave despite some condemnation of his summing up of the case, Edward Seton is hanged for murder in Agatha Christie's bestselling whodunnit *And Then There Were None*.

11

1965: After a reading at the alternative independent London bookshop Better Books in Charing Cross Road the previous month, Allen Ginsberg leads a who's who of young modern male poets at the International Poetry Incarnation. Held at the Royal Albert Hall, this poetry reading is held in front of 7,000 people, who are handed flowers as they enter. Among those taking part in the loosely organised four-hour performance are Beat poets Ginsberg (who reads Andrei Vosnesensky's 'New York Bird'), William S. Burroughs, Gregory Corso, Lawrence Ferlinghetti, Christopher Logue, George MacBeth and Adrian Mitchell (who reads his anti-Vietnam, anti-fake news poem 'To Whom It May Concern'). Pablo Neruda is due to read, but cancels, and the Russian Vosnesensky is in the line-up but prohibited by minders from the Russian embassy from performing. The event, sometimes regarded as the first 'happening', helps coalesce the growing counter-culture movement in the UK and the *Times Literary Supplement* comments a week later that the event has 'made literary history by a combination of flair, courage, and seized opportunities'.

12

1850: William Thackeray throws a dinner party for Charlotte Brontë at his home in London. They are both admirers of each other's work – indeed he is one of the literary heroes to whom she dedicated the second edition of *Jane Eyre*. But their relationship has already gone slightly awry at a previous meeting (see 4 December). On this day, the dinner party is equally awkward. The other invited guests are female writers, but Charlotte is shy and conversation doesn't flow. Asked by novelist and literary hostess Jane Brookfield if she likes London, there is a long pause before Charlotte replies: 'Yes … No.' She leaves early, quickly followed by Thackeray, who heads to his club.

1863: Anthony Trollope and Charles Dickens are among the co-founders of the Arts Club in Mayfair, attracting many famous practitioners of the creative arts. Other writers who become members include Wilkie Collins and Thomas Hughes. This is how Dickens's son, Charles Dickens Jr, describes its mission in his 1879 *Dictionary of London*: 'This club is instituted for the purpose of facilitating the social intercourse of those connected with, or interested in, art literature, or science. Candidates for membership must have a bona fide qualification.'

1942: On her thirteenth birthday in Amsterdam, just after 7 a.m., Anne Frank receives a red-and-white chequered diary as a present.

13

1966: It's a full day for Dame Muriel Spark. Her diary shows her booked in for a haircut at Elizabeth Arden at 10.30 a.m., then a French lesson at 3 p.m., and finally dinner at 7.15 p.m. with publisher Alfred Knopf.

14

1966: Pope Paul VI finally puts an end to the Vatican's *Index Librorum Prohibitorum*, an ongoing record of literature banned from being bought, sold, published, kept, passed on, translated and, of course, read on grounds of morality or being heretical. The Index was established in 1559. While some bans were of single works, others were of everything an author had written. Anybody breaking the ban faced excommunication from the Catholic Church. The Index featured many writers of fiction over its four centuries of life, as well as theologians and philosophers, including Francis Bacon, Voltaire, Honoré de Balzac, Alexandre Dumas (*père* and *fils*), Victor Hugo, John Milton, George Sand, André Gide and Jean-Paul Sartre. The final list was published in 1948, though additions were made for another thirteen years. The Sacred Congregation for the Doctrine of the Faith, which administers the Index, says in its Notification regarding the abolition of the index of books issued on this day that 'the Index remains morally binding ... But, at the same time, it no longer has the force of ecclesiastical law with the attached censure.'

15

1784: Dr Johnson comments to Boswell on the advice of a certain Reverend Herbert Croft to a former pupil that if you start a book then you should always finish it. 'This is surely a strange advice,' grumbles Johnson. 'You may as well resolve that whatever men you happen to get acquainted with, you are to keep to them for life. A book may be good for nothing; or there may be only one thing in it worth knowing; are we to read it all through? These *Voyages* (pointing to

the three large volumes of *Voyages to the South Sea* which were just come out), who will read them through? A man had better work his way before the mast, than read them through; they will be eaten by rats and mice, before they are read through.'

1815: Three days before the Battle of Waterloo and on the eve of the Battle of Quatre Bras, the Duchess of Richmond holds a ball in Brussels. Invitees include royalty, aristocracy, ambassadors, generals and officers of the Duke of Wellington's army, but the ball ends suddenly with news that Napoleon's forces are advancing. The ball has a tremendous literary afterlife, featuring in, among others, William Thackeray's *Vanity Fair* (Becky Sharp is in a particularly charming mood), *Childe Harold's Pilgrimage* by Lord Byron, *An Infamous Army* by Georgette Heyer, Bernard Cornwell's *Sharpe's Waterloo* and *Belgravia* by Julian Fellowes.

16

1904: The day on which the events of James Joyce's *Ulysses* take place, celebrated annually as Bloomsday. The first such commemoration is held in 1954 by Dublin writers including Brian O'Nolan (aka Flann O'Brien aka Myles na Gopaleen), Patrick Kavanagh and Anthony Cronin. Their booze-fuelled tour of the book's route, partly in horse-drawn cabs, is immortalised in a sixty-second piece of footage available freely online in which O'Nolan is barely vertical.

It's also an important date for Joyce romantically. On 10 June 1904 he meets Nora Barnacle, later to become his muse and wife. They arrange to rendezvous on 14 June but she fails to turn up. He writes to her on 15 June saying he is 'quite dejected' and asking if they can rearrange. And on this day they have their first proper date.

Vir vere magnus!
Nomen in exemplum sero
Servabimus ævo!

AN
Historical Account
OF THE
BATTLE
OF
WATERLOO.

Dyer sculp.

Etch'd by G. Cruikshank.

Publish'd by H. Colburn, Conduit Street, London, 1816.

Rouse sculp.

17

1924: 'Worked all day,' Enid Blyton writes in her diary. Her work log indicates that she wrote the poem 'Silver and Gold', which is the first in the collection of the same name that comes out the following year. The short diary entry ends with a note that she went out to dinner at a friend's, where they played slapdown, perhaps the Slap-Down Patience game mentioned in her 1945 *Five Go to Smuggler's Top*.

18

1746: Dr Samuel Johnson is breakfasting in the Golden Anchor tavern in Holborn, London, with a group of printer-booksellers who are urging him to sign a contract to produce a dictionary. Initially reluctant, he realises he really does want to take it on after all when they offer him the enormous sum of 1,500 guineas (£1,575). Johnson estimates it will take him three years, but it is a bigger task than he expects and is not published until 15 April 1755.

1956: Irish playwright Brendan Behan turns up for a BBC *Panorama* interview with Malcolm Muggeridge absolutely plastered on Scotch. Things are not improved when he continues drinking whisky before the interview in the green room, where he gets overly friendly with several debutantes who are his fellow guests. During the interview, in which he swears, he wears no shoes, becomes increasingly unkempt and ends up by 'singing' the song 'The Auld Triangle' by his drinking buddy Dick Shannon. Unfortunately, no tapes of the transmission survive, although Peter Sellers immortalises it in a comic 'recreation' called 'In a Free State' which is available online.

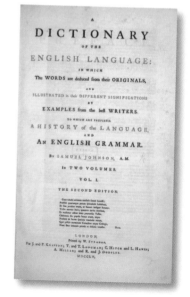

19

528: Hank leaps back through time from 1879 to Camelot in Mark Twain's 1889 *A Yankee in King Arthur's Court.*

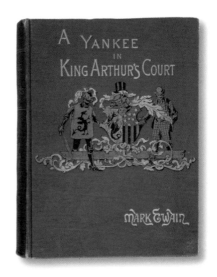

20

1914: Modernist literary arts magazine *Blast* launches its first edition (dated today, but actually not out until 2 July). The short-lived periodical of the Vorticist movement, the magazine is the work of writers Wyndham Lewis and Ezra Pound and includes a manifesto for Vorticism, plus a play by Lewis, fiction by Rebecca West and Ford Madox Ford, and various 'blasts' and 'curses' ('Curse the flabby sky that can manufacture no snow but can only drop the sea on us in drizzle like a poem by Mr Robert Bridges').

21

1968: Ursula K. Le Guin's literary agent Virginia Kidd receives the following letter from an editor who has been sent the manuscript for *The Left Hand of Darkness*, later a hugely popular bestseller:

'Ursula K. Le Guin writes extremely well, but I'm sorry to have to say that on the basis of that one highly distinguishing quality alone I cannot make you an offer for the novel. The book is so endlessly complicated by details of reference and information, the interim legends become so much of a nuisance despite their relevance, that the very action of the story seems to me to become hopelessly bogged down and the book, eventually, unreadable. The whole is so dry and airless, so lacking in pace, that whatever drama and excitement the novel might have had is entirely dissipated by what does seem, a great deal of the time, to be extraneous material. My thanks nonetheless for having thought of us. The manuscript of *The Left Hand of Darkness* is returned herewith.'

Decades later Le Guin adds it to her website but omits the name of the editor and publishing house 'because I am a very kind person'.

22

1484: Anna Rügerin from Augsburg, Germany, becomes the first recorded woman to include her name as the printer in a book's colophon, the section that includes details about the author and the date when the title was produced. The book is a medieval handbook to German law called the *Sachsenspiegel*. She prints a second volume on 29 July, an instruction manual for editing official documents.

23

1659: America's first female poet, Anne Bradstreet (1612–1672), writes 'In Reference to Her Children, 23 June 1659', the earliest known poem about empty nester parents' feelings:

I had eight birds hatcht in one nest,
Four Cocks were there, and Hens the rest.
I nurst them up with pain and care,
No cost nor labour did I spare
Till at the last they felt their wing,
Mounted the Trees and learned to sing.
Chief of the Brood then took his flight
To Regions far and left me quite.
My mournful chirps I after send
Till he return, or I do end.

Leave not thy nest, thy Dame and Sire,
Fly back and sing amidst this Quire.
My second bird did take her flight
And with her mate flew out of sight.
Southward they both their course did bend,

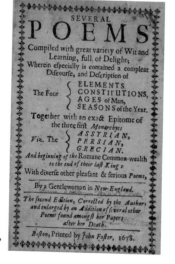

And Seasons twain they there did spend,
Till after blown by Southern gales
They Norward steer'd with filled sails.
A prettier bird was no where seen,
Along the Beach, among the treen.

I have a third of colour white
On whom I plac'd no small delight,
Coupled with mate loving and true,
Hath also bid her Dame adieu.
And where Aurora first appears,
She now hath percht to spend her years.

One to the Academy flew
To chat among that learned crew.
Ambition moves still in his breast
That he might chant above the rest,
Striving for more than to do well,
That nightingales he might excell.

My fifth, whose down is yet scarce gone,
Is 'mongst the shrubs and bushes flown
And as his wings increase in strength
On higher boughs he'll perch at length.
My other three still with me nest
Until they're grown, then as the rest,
Or here or there, they'll take their flight,
As is ordain'd, so shall they light.

If birds could weep, then would my tears
Let others know what are my fears
Lest this my brood some harm should catch
And be surpris'd for want of watch
Whilst pecking corn and void of care
They fall un'wares in Fowler's snare;
Or whilst on trees they sit and sing
Some untoward boy at them do fling,

Or whilst allur'd with bell and glass
The net be spread and caught, alas;
Or lest by Lime-twigs they be foil'd;
Or by some greedy hawks be spoil'd.

O would, my young, ye saw my breast
And knew what thoughts there sadly rest.
Great was my pain when I you bred,
Great was my care when I you fed.
Long did I keep you soft and warm
And with my wings kept off all harm.
My cares are more, and fears, than ever,
My throbs such now as 'fore were never.

Alas, my birds, you wisdom want
Of perils you are ignorant.
Oft times in grass, on trees, in flight,
Sore accidents on you may light.
O to your safety have an eye,
So happy may you live and die.
Mean while, my days in tunes I'll spend
Till my weak lays with me shall end.
In shady woods I'll sit and sing
And things that past, to mind I'll bring.
Once young and pleasant, as are you,
But former toys (no joys) adieu!

My age I will not once lament
But sing, my time so near is spent,
And from the top bough take my flight
Into a country beyond sight
Where old ones instantly grow young
And there with seraphims set song.
No seasons cold, nor storms they see
But spring lasts to eternity.

When each of you shall in your nest
Among your young ones take your rest,
In chirping languages oft them tell
You had a Dame that lov'd you well,
That did what could be done for young
And nurst you up till you were strong
And 'fore she once would let you fly
She shew'd you joy and misery,
Taught what was good, and what was ill,
What would save life, and what would kill.

Thus gone, amongst you I may live,
And dead, yet speak and counsel give.
Farewell, my birds, farewell, adieu,
I happy am, if well with you.

1944: Novelist Rumer Godden, living in India, discovers that she and
her children are being poisoned by her Kashmiri cook, who has been
putting ground glass and opium in their food in a bizarre attempt to
both seduce and kill her. The Goddens escape unscathed, but their
dog dies. 'Life has been like an Agatha Christie,' she writes to her
sister, Jon. She fictionalises the incident in her humorous 1953 novel
Kingfishers Catch Fire.

24

1914: At 12.45, poet Edward Thomas's Paddington to Malvern train
stops at Adlestrop station on the Cotswold Line in Gloucestershire (a
scheduled stop rather than an unexpected one). He makes a record of
it in his notebook, which features in the poem of the same name he
later writes – probably in January 1915 – about the journey:

'Then we stopped at Adlestrop, through the willows could be heard a
chain of blackbirds' songs at 12:45 and one thrush and no man seen,
only a hiss of engine letting off steam. Stopping outside Campden by
banks of long willowherb and meadowsweet, extraordinary silence
between the two periods of travel – looking out on grey dry stones
between metals and shining metals and over it all the elms willows

and long grass – one man clears his throat – and a great, greater rustic silence. No house in view. Stop only for a minute till the signal is up.'

Thomas is killed on 9 April 1917, at the Battle of Arras, three weeks before 'Adlestrop' is printed in the *New Statesman* magazine.

25

Rosemary Woodhouse has her baby in *Rosemary's Baby* (1967) by Ira Levin.

26

1284: The Pied Piper, unwisely brushed off by the Hamelin authorities after saving them from a plague of rats, follows through on his threat that folks who put him in a passion may find him pipe to another fashion. He turns his attention to the children of the town and leads them away, as a plaque in English on the building known as the *Rattenfängerhaus* (Rat Catcher's House) or the Pied Piper's House recounts:

Tripping and skipping, ran merrily after

The wonderful music with shouting and laughter

'AD 1284 – on the 26th of June – the day of St John and St Paul – 130 children – born in Hamelin – were led out of the town by a piper wearing multicoloured clothes. After passing the Calvary near the Koppenberg they disappeared forever.'

It is not clear why such a specific date is mentioned, but it does closely correlate to other documention in the town's records about the children's disappearance.

1963: Penelope Fitzgerald's girls had woken up on 24 June to find water in their bedroom on board the family canal boat, *Grace*, where they have been living since 1960. *Grace* finally sinks on this day and Fitzgerald loses many family possessions, letters and photographs. Some books are salvaged, though damaged.

27

It is the day of the lottery in 'The Lottery' by Shirley Jackson, set in her home town of North Bennington, Vermont. Her short story is first published on 26 June 1948 in the *New Yorker* and the magazine is immediately flooded with letters of complaint.

1787: Between 11 p.m. and midnight in a Lausanne summerhouse, Edward Gibbon writes the final lines of his magnum opus, *The Decline and Fall of the Roman Empire*. He describes it as 'the hour of my deliverance':

'After laying down my pen I took several turns in a berceau, or covered walk of acacias, which commands a prospect of the country, the lake, and the mountains. The air was temperate, the sky was serene, the silver orb of the moon was reflected from the waters, and all nature was silent. I will not dissemble the first emotions of joy on recovery of my freedom, and, perhaps, the establishment of my fame. But my pride was soon humbled, and a sober melancholy was spread over my mind, by the idea that I had taken an everlasting leave of an old and agreeable companion.'

In 1897, Thomas Hardy visits the location and writes his poem 'Lausanne: In Gibbon's Old Garden', on which he adds the date of its creation: 'The 110th anniversary of the completion of the *Decline and Fall* at the same hour and place'.

1928: Shakespeare and Company bookshop founder Sylvia Beach hosts a dinner party for friends, largely with the aim of introducing F. Scott Fitzgerald to James Joyce since he is nervous about contacting the author of *Ulysses*. Fitzgerald draws a picture of those in attendance in Beach's copy of *The Great Gatsby*, with Beach as a mermaid and Joyce sporting a halo. He also (probably) kneels in front of Joyce and asks: 'How does it feel to be a great genius, Sir?'

28

1932: Peter Llewelyn Davies (J. M. Barrie's inspiration for Peter Pan) and Alice Hargreaves née Liddell (Lewis Carroll's inspiration for Alice) meet at a centenary exhibition celebrating Carroll's birth in London bookshop Bumpus. There is no record of their conversation, although Davies has increasingly come to dislike his public association with the Pan character.

American playwright John Logan writes a fictionalised account of their meeting, *Peter and Alice*, which opens at the Noël Coward Theatre in London on 13 March 2013. It stars Judi Dench as Alice and Ben Whishaw as Peter. 'We're practically our own children's department,' says Alice in the play.

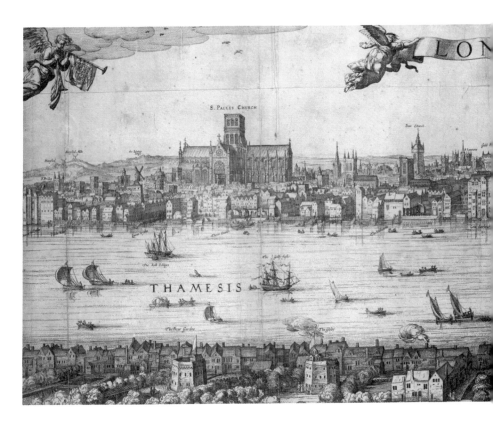

29

1613: Shakespeare's Globe Theatre burns to the ground during an afternoon performance of his play *All Is True* (now known as *Henry VIII* and co-written with John Fletcher) when the special effects team fire small cannons towards the end of Act I and accidentally set fire to the thatched roof. It burns down in an hour. On 2 July, writer and politician Sir Henry Wotton writes to Sir Edmund Bacon describing the fire, which he says 'ran round like a train', adding: 'This was the fatal period of that vertuous fabrique, wherein yet nothing did perish, but wood and straw, and a few forsaken cloaks; only one man had his breeches set on fire, that would perhaps have broyled him, if he had not by the benefit of a provident wit put it out with bottle Ale.'

1885: Former architect Thomas Hardy moves in to Max Gate, the house he has designed himself in Dorchester and which is built by his brother Henry. It has taken two years to build and is within walking distance of his childhood cottage home at nearby Higher Bockhampton.

30

1943: Jack Kerouac officially receives his honourable discharge from the US Navy on psychiatric grounds after suffering a series of headaches.

FINAL WORDS

'Beautiful.'
Elizabeth Barrett Browning (29 June 1861)

'On the ground.'
Charles Dickens (9 June 1870)

'I can't sleep.'
J. M. Barrie (19 June 1937)

'Too late for fruit, too soon for flowers.'
Walter de la Mare (22 June 1956), being asked which he would prefer

'Here lies Malcolm Lowry, late of the Bowery, whose prose was flowery, and often glowery. He lived nightly, and drank daily, and died playing the ukulele.'
Malcolm Lowry (26 June 1957), his self-penned epitaph

JULY

The English winter – ending in July,
To recommence in August – now was done
Don Juan (1819) by Lord Byron

Births
Barbara Cartland (9 July 1901)
John Wyndham (10 July 1903)
Pablo Neruda (13 July 1904)
Denys Watkins-Pitchford – 'BB' (25 July 1905)
Wendy Cope (21 July 1945)

Deaths
Jane Austen (18 July 1817)
Guy de Maupassant (6 July 1893)
Carol Shields (16 July 2003)
Paula Danziger (8 July 2004)
Nadine Gordimer (13 July 2014)

First published/performed
7 July 1814: *Waverley* by Sir Walter Scott
4 July 1855: *Leaves of Grass* by Walt Whitman
29 July 1935: *Seven Pillars of Wisdom* by T. E. Lawrence
16 July 1951: *The Catcher in the Rye* by J. D. Salinger
11 July 1960: *To Kill a Mockingbird* by Harper Lee

1

1973: The British Library is born, following the implementation of the 1972 British Library Act (see 24 November). Previously it had been the British Museum Library, which was founded in 1753.

2

1916: Field Marshal Douglas Haig notes that the previous day, the first in the Battle of the Somme, was 'a day of downs and ups', going on to note that:

'I visit two casualty-clearing stations. They were very pleased at my visit, the wounded were in wonderful spirits. Reported today that total casualties are estimated at over 40,000. This cannot be considered severe in view of numbers engaged and the length of front of attack. By nightfall the situation is much more favourable than when we started today.'

3

1767: Captain Philip Carteret sights, describes and names Pitcairn Island in his journal:

'We continued our course westward till the evening of Thursday the 2d of July, when we discovered land to the northward of us. Upon approaching it the next day, it appeared like a great rock rising out of the sea: it was not more than five miles in circumference, and seemed to be uninhabited; it was, however, covered with trees, and we saw a small stream of fresh water running down one side of it. I would have landed upon it, but the surf, which at this season broke upon it with great violence, rendered it impossible. I got soundings on the west side of it, at somewhat less than a mile from the shore, in twenty-five fathom, with a bottom of coral and sand; and it is probable that in fine summer weather landing here may not only be practicable but easy. We saw a great number of sea birds hovering about it, at somewhat less than a mile from the shore, and the sea

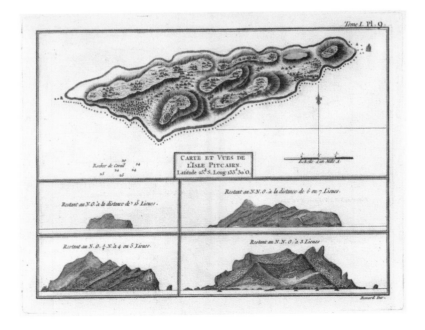

here seemed to have fish. It lies in
latitude 25° 2' S., longitude 133° 21'
W. and about a thousand leagues
to the westward of the continent
of America. It is so high that
we saw it at the distance of
more than fifteen leagues, and
it having been discovered by a
young gentleman, son to Major
Pitcairn of the marines, who was
unfortunately lost in the Aurora, we
called it PITCAIRN'S ISLAND.'

1834: Businesswoman and mountaineer
Anne Lister – also known as Gentleman Jack – has become well
known in recent years thanks to her detailed and often very personal
diaries: her relationship with Ann Walker resulted in what is
sometimes described as Britain's first lesbian wedding. Walker too
kept a diary. On this day they are travelling together in Europe. Lister
describes in considerable detail in more than 500 words (some of
them in her secret code) what time she gets up and goes to bed, the
temperature, the details and history of their hotel, how she manages to
smuggle some handkerchiefs through customs, the worsening weather,
her roast veal dinner, and what time she spends together with Walker.
Walker manages the same day in a more succinct twenty words.

4

1862: Lewis Carroll tells the story of what will become *Alice's
Adventures in Wonderland* for the first time to the young Alice Liddell
and her sisters as they enjoy a boat trip down the river in Oxford.
His diary reveals:

July 4 (F) Atkinson brought over to my rooms some friends of his,
a Mrs & Miss Peters, of whom I took photographs, & who afterwards
looked over my albums & staid to lunch. They then went off to
the Museum, & Duckworth & I made an expedition up the river to

Godstow with the 3 Liddells: we had tea on the bank there, & did not reach Ch. Ch. Again till ¼ past 8, when we took them on to my rooms to see my collection of micro-photographs, & restored them to the Deanery just before 9.'

In an addition to the entry on the opposite page, he says:

'On which occasion I told them the fairy-tale of 'Alice's Adventures Under Ground', which I undertook to write out for Alice, & which is now finished (as to the text) though the pictures are not yet nearly done – Feb. 10. 1863
nor yet – Mar. 12. 1864.
'Alice's Hour in Elfland'? June 9/64.
~~Alice's~~ Adventures in Wonderland'? June 28.'

5

1925: Having enjoyed *The Great Gatsby*, Edith Wharton invites F. Scott Fitzgerald to tea along with her friend, the American composer Teddy Chanler. Rather nervous, Fitzgerald characteristically indulges too much in Dutch courage and turns up a bit tired and emotional (and without his wife Zelda, who feels she would be rather out of place at such a grand gathering). To enliven the slightly dull afternoon, Fitzgerald tells a story about living in a brothel which sinks like a lead balloon. As Wharton puts it in her diary later that day: 'To tea, Teddy Chanler and Scott Fitzgerald, the novelist (awful).'

6

1945: Lawyer and military administrator Denis Capel-Dunn dies in a plane crash off Newfoundland. He is a major inspiration for Kenneth Widmerpool, a key character in the novel sequence *A Dance to the Music of Time* by Anthony Powell (who has served under him during the Second World War).

7

1809: After several years in Bath, where her writing has hit something of a wall, Jane Austen moves with her mother and sister Cassandra to the quiet Hampshire village of Chawton. Set up in a house by her brother Edward, Jane begins writing seriously again.

8

1848: Having caught a night train down from their home in Yorkshire the previous evening, Charlotte and Anne Brontë arrive in London unannounced to clear up with their publishers the knotty issue of their true identity. Despite only planning initially to stay one night, they enjoy a visit to the Royal Opera House (then the Royal Italian Opera) in the evening, which Charlotte recounts in her letter of 4 September that year to her friend Mary Taylor:

'The performance was Rossini's opera of the Barber of Seville, very brilliant, though I fancy there are things I should like better. We got home after one o'clock; we had never been in bed the night before, and had been in constant excitement for twenty-four hours. You may imagine we were tired.'

They continue to enjoy London over the next few days, going to a service at St Stephen's Church in Walbrook, wandering around the capital's parks, going shopping and enjoying exhibitions at the Royal Academy and National Gallery. At dinner one evening, they are entertained by the singing of one of Leigh Hunt's daughters.

2013: A twelve-foot fibreglass model of the moment in the 1995 BBC adaption of *Pride and Prejudice* when Colin Firth's Mr Darcy emerges wet-shirted from a lake is installed in London's Serpentine lake. Essentially a piece of PR to promote a new television channel, the statue then goes on a tour of the UK before settling down in Melbourne, Australia. The scene of course does not feature in Jane Austen's novel, only in Andrew Davies' script.

9

1927: One of the most famous fictional pigs, the Empress of Blandings, makes her debut in the US magazine *Liberty* in a short story by P. G. Wodehouse, 'Pig-hoo-o-o-o-ey'. The story of Lord Emsworth's pride and joy comes out in the UK in the August edition of the *Strand Magazine*.

10

1958: There's a fascinating chat on the BBC Home Service today between Raymond Chandler and Ian Fleming. They naturally discuss their respective creations Philip Marlowe and James Bond, and the difference between English and American thrillers (though Fleming describes Chandler's work as 'novels of suspense'). But Chandler, of whom Fleming is obviously slightly in awe, also shows himself knowledgeable about exactly how to perform a mafia hit and says that 'I know what it is to be banged on the head with a revolver butt. The first thing you do is vomit.' Talking about Bond, Fleming admits: 'On the whole I think he's a rather unattractive man.'

11

1818: On a summer walking tour, the twenty-two-year-old John Keats visits Robert Burns's first home in Alloway, Scotland. 'I am approaching Burns's cottage very fast,' he writes to his friend John Reynolds on this day.

'We have made continual enquiries from the time we left his tomb at Dumfries. His name, of course, is known all about: his great reputation among the plodding people is, "that he wrote a good mony [sic] sensible things". One of the pleasantest ways of annulling self is approaching such a shrine as the Cottage of Burns: we need not think of his misery – that is all gone, bad luck to it! I shall look upon it hereafter with unmixed pleasure.'

While he is there, Keats writes his accurately titled sonnet 'Written in the Cottage Where Burns Was Born':

This mortal body of a thousand days
Now fills, O Burns, a space in thine own room,
Where thou didst dream alone on budded bays,
Happy and thoughtless of thy day of doom!
My pulse is warm with thine old barley-bree,
My head is light with pledging a great soul,
My eyes are wandering, and I cannot see,
Fancy is dead and drunken at its goal;
Yet can I stamp my foot upon thy floor,
Yet can I ope thy window-sash to find
The meadow thou hast tramped o'er and o'er; –
Yet can I think of thee till thought is blind, –
Yet can I gulp a bumper to thy name, –
O smile among the shades, for this is fame!

2019: Dublin-born Iris Murdoch's birth centenary (actually falling on 15 July) is celebrated in Ireland by An Post with the issue of a postage stamp of the novelist designed by Steve Simpson. The design features her portrait in the style of her early book covers.

12

1932: J. L. Carr, author of *A Month in the Country* and a cricket fanatic, misses Yorkshire's Hedley Verity bowling Nottinghamshire out for just sixty-seven, Verity taking a remarkable ten for ten. Carr claims he was at the Headingley ground that morning with his brother-in-law, but it is a bit drizzly and his companion forecasts that rain will stop play for the day, so persuades him to leave and catch an early train back to Sherburn in Elmet. However, it doesn't rain, and Hedley Verity wins the day. Carr later says missing this feat 'blighted my youth'.

13

1941: Cartoonist Ronald Searle, called up to serve in the army, is staying in the village of Kirkcudbright, Scotland. During one of his regular visits to local friends, he draws a cartoon for their two daughters Cécilé and Pat Johnston. They are enjoying their time as pupils at the somewhat experimental nearby school, an academy for young ladies, called St Trinnean's. This is the first of his many St Trinian's cartoons – it shows various schoolgirls looking at their school noticeboard and is captioned 'Owing to the international situation, the match with St Trinian's has been postponed.' Searle is pleased with how it turns out and submits it on this day to Kaye Webb, assistant editor at *Lilliput* magazine (whom he will later marry). *Lilliput* publishes the cartoon in October but before then Searle is posted to Singapore. He sees it entirely by accident on 13 February 1942, when he comes across it among some rubbish in the city, at that point under Japanese fire.

1930: Six days after his death on 7 July, the Spiritualist Association rents the Royal Albert Hall for a largely free memorial séance for Sir Arthur Conan Doyle (7 p.m., doors open 6.15 p.m.). It's an event that

will feature in Julian Barnes's novel *Arthur & George* (2005). In front of a packed audience of around 6,000 people – hundreds more are turned away when the hall reaches capacity – celebrated medium Estelle Roberts tries to put the keen spiritualist and Sherlock Holmes creator in touch with his widow and family.

Roberts and the family claim success and that Sir Arthur appears, apparently dressed for the occasion in evening clothes, sits down in a vacant chair placed there specifically for him, and talks about people visiting his hut earlier in the day. He then passes on a jolly message to Lady Conan Doyle (which she declines to reveal, as it is personal). A reporter for the *Saturday Review* newspaper suggests that the evidence of the triumph would not satisfy Watson, let alone Holmes.

1951: Novelist Sylvia Townsend Warner, author of *Lolly Willowes*, spends the day making a blue and white nightgown, and mending some linen sheets. She also mentions in her diary that, taking a look at the size of her bank balance after completing her tax return, she feels 'quite faint' (in a good way) at its size.

14

1077: The Bayeux Tapestry probably goes on display for the first time as decoration for the town's cathedral during its consecration on this day. Likely to have been commissioned by Bishop Odo, William the Conqueror's half-brother and regent of England, the tapestry has Anglo-Saxon elements in the Latin titles, or 'tituli', that accompany the images – suggesting it may have been made in England.

1989: *When Harry Met Sally* – written by Nora Ephron, directed by Rob Reiner and starring Billy Crystal, Meg Ryan and Carrie Fisher – is released. At one point, Harry (played by Crystal) is seen reading *Misery* by Stephen King. He is right at the beginning but skips suddenly to the last page, confirming what he has admitted at the start of the film: 'When I buy a new book, I always read the last page first; that way in case I die before I finish, I know how it ends.' *Misery* becomes the next book adaptation filmed by Reiner.

15

1677 or 1684: For his brave services, Marlinspike Hall is bestowed on Captain Haddock's ancestor Francis (François de Hadoque, in the original French). In the translated English edition of the Tintin adventure *Red Rackham's Treasure*, this clearly happens in 1677 as a gift from the English monarch Charles II. But matters are complicated since in the original French edition, *Le Trésor de Rackham le Rouge*, the grant deeds pictured suggest that the date is in fact 1684 and the king is obviously the French Louis XIV.

16

1951: It's publication day for J. D. Salinger's *The Catcher in the Rye* and the first reviews for what is already a popular hit are in. Indeed the previous day James Stern, in the *New York Times*, likes it so much he writes the entire review in the style of Holden Caulfield's voice, and Paul Engle for the Chicago *Sunday Tribune* hails it as 'emotional without being sentimental, dramatic without being melodramatic, and honest without simply being obscene'. There are of course some dissenting voices. Virgilia Peterson in the *New York Herald Tribune Book Review* feels that: 'Recent war novels have accustomed us all to ugly words and images, but from the mouths of the very young and protected they sound peculiarly offensive.' However, on this day, *Time* magazine enthuses: 'He can understand an adolescent mind without displaying one,' while the *New York Times* has a second bite of the cherry via Nash K. Burger, who says that 'Mr Salinger's rendering of teen-age speech is wonderful'.

1961: Evelyn Waugh takes a major step in the restoration of P. G. Wodehouse's reputation following his poorly considered but also badly misunderstood series of broadcasts while under Nazi house arrest in Berlin. Waugh publishes his 'An Act of Homage and Reparation' in today's *Sunday Times*, a version of the radio address he has made the previous evening on the BBC Home Service. He claims the attacks on Wodehouse are largely 'not on grounds of patriotism but of class'. 'Three full generations have delighted in Mr Wodehouse,' he continues. 'He satisfies the most sophisticated taste and the simplest.'

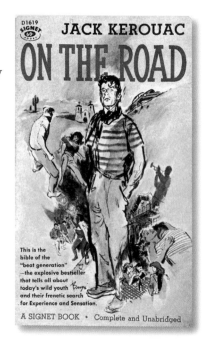

17

1947: The twenty-five-year-old Jack Kerouac sets off on a road trip across the US, planning to travel from his home in Ozone Park, New York via Denver to San Francisco and to meet up with friends Allen Ginsberg and Neal Cassady along the way. His journals and notes from this trip inspire his novel *On the Road*.

18

1917: Despite fighting at the battles of Passchendaele and the Somme, the illustrator E. H. Shepard escapes from the First World War unhurt. On this day, his bravery is recognised with an announcement in the *London Gazette* that he is awarded the Military Cross:

'His Majesty the King has been graciously pleased to confer the Military Cross on the undermentioned Officers and Warrant Officers in recognition of their gallantry and devotion to duty in the Field. For conspicuous gallantry and devotion to duty. As forward Observation Officer he [E. H. Shepard] continued to observe and send back valuable information, in spite of heavy shell and machine gun fire. His courage and coolness were conspicuous.'

1925: Playwright Samuel Beckett makes his debut in first-class cricket playing for Dublin University away against Northamptonshire at the County Ground in Northampton. He scores eighteen runs in the first innings and twelve in the second. He also bowls eight overs for an economical seventeen runs, two maidens and no wickets, as Northamptonshire win by an innings and fifty-six runs. Beckett's second and final first-class appearance is in the same fixture the following year on 7 July. Northamptonshire make 454 in their first innings, during which Beckett takes a couple of catches, and bowls fifteen overs, again wicketless, for forty-seven runs (one maiden). He only manages to score four and one in his two innings, bowled both times.

19

1957: Evelyn Waugh publishes his partly autobiographical novel *The Ordeal of Gilbert Pinfold* today. He also rather reluctantly goes to a Foyle's Literary Lunch to publicise it, but enlivens the event by explaining: 'Three years ago, I had quite a new experience. I went off my head for about three weeks.' Malcolm Muggeridge also gives a speech and Waugh very ostentatiously dismantles his telescopic spoon-shaped copper Victorian ear trumpet during his oration, rather discomfiting the speaker.

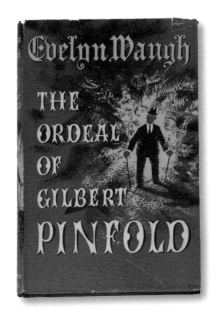

The eighteen-inch trumpet, described by his son Auberon as 'a disgusting object', sells for £2,200 at auction in 2017.

20

1841: After four years in the High Beach asylum in Epping Forest, John Clare absconds and begins a ninety-mile, four-day walk back to his East Midlands home in Northborough, Cambridgeshire. He writes an account of his journey, and on this day:

'I missed the lane to Enfield Town, and was going down Enfield Highway, till I passed the 'Labour-in-vain' public-house, where a person who came out of the door told me the way. I walked down the lane gently, and was soon in Enfield Town, and by and by on the great York Road, where it was all plain sailing. Steering ahead, meeting no enemy and fearing none, I reached Stevenage, where, being night, I got over a gate, and crossed the corner of a green paddock. Seeing a pond or hollow in the corner, I was forced to stay off a respectable distance to keep from falling into it. My legs were nearly knocked up and began to stagger. I scaled over some old rotten palings into the yard, and then had higher palings to clamber over, to get into the shed or hovel; which I did with difficulty, being rather weak. To my good luck, I found some trusses of clover piled up, about six or more feet square, which I gladly mounted and slept on. There were some drags in the hovel, on which I could have reposed had I not found a better bed. I slept soundly, but had a very uneasy dream. I thought my first wife lay on my left arm, and somebody took her away from my side, which made me wake up rather unhappy. I thought as I awoke somebody said 'Mary', but nobody was near. I lay down with my head towards the north, to show myself the steering point in the morning.'

At Christmas time, when his mental health does not improve, he is committed to the Northampton General Lunatic Asylum, where he lives, fairly comfortably, for the rest of his life.

1916: Robert Graves is so badly wounded by an exploding bomb at the Battle of the Somme that his family are told he has died and an announcement of his demise appears in *The Times*. It acknowledges its error on 5 August on its Court Circular page:

... the shrub the blithy boult
the grasshopper chirps his note
Bounding on from stalk to stalk

While the bee at early hours
sips the dawny beans perfume
butterflys infest the flowers
first to show their glossy plumes

Soft industry seeks the sweet
which weary labour oft to gain
oft the bliss the idle meets
leaven bestows the step in vain

Pleasd I list the rural themes
... up the ploughmans toil
... the jingling teams
They turn the yellow soil

Industrys care abounds again
now the peace of night is gone
... a murmur wakes the plain
... a waggon rumbles on

... swallow wheels his curling flight
oer the waters surface skims
... the cottage chimney lights
... merry chaunts his morning hymns

... high a towering height
... the sun gilt weather cock
... the jackdaw takes his flight
... by the striking clock

... the wary watching thrush
... to hunne her speckled breast
... the woodbine round the bush
... hides her mortard nest

... the cows with hungry low
... the rank grass from her bower

'Captain Robert Graves, Royal Welsh Fusiliers, officially reported died of wounds, wishes to inform his friends that he is recovering from his wounds at Queen Alexandra's Hospital, Highgate.'

21

2021: It's the final day of the Sotheby's auction featuring Sylvia Plath's letters to Ted Hughes. Plath was a keen cook, and the sale also includes various of her culinary possessions, including her rolling pin ('incised with decorative figures, painted handles, 405mm, *chipped'*) and thirty-three of her recipe cards featuring 'Clara's Basic Yeast Dough', 'Ted's mother's Scots porridge oats biscuits' and 'Grammy's Fish Chowder'. The two lots are eventually sold together for £20,160.

22

1941: It's Eugene O'Neill's twelfth wedding anniversary. His present to his wife, Carlotta, is his final draft of *Long Day's Journey into Night*. He has just finished it and dedicates it to her:

Dearest: I give you the original script of this play of old sorrow, written in tears and blood. A sadly inappropriate gift, it would seem, for a day celebrating happiness. But you will understand. I mean it as a tribute to your love and tenderness which gave me the faith in love that enabled me to face my dead at last and write this play – write it with deep pity and understanding and forgiveness for all the four haunted Tyrones. These twelve years, Beloved One, have been a Journey into Light – into love … You know my gratitude. And my love!

23

1934: Keen socialist H. G. Wells spends three hours in Moscow interviewing the leader of the Soviet Union, Joseph Stalin, for the *New Statesman* magazine. The interview goes reasonably well, covering issues such as class war, international relations and freedom of expression. Stalin is a little prickly and has a tendency to speak in platitudinous soundbites, while Wells suggests that he himself appears

WHEN YOU'RE A LONG, LONG WAY FROM HOME (1).
I know where the sun is shining, I know where someone is pining,
Just a simple pal, a country gal, I know she's true ;
What's the use of tears and sighing ? After many years of trying,
Guess I'm going home no more to roam, I'm feeling blue.

BY ARRANGEMENT WITH MESSRS. FRANCIS, DAY & HUNTER, THE PUBLISHERS OF THE MUSIC
BAMFORTH COPYRIGHT

to be more left wing than the general secretary of the Communist Party. Here are the opening salvos:

Wells: I am very much obliged to you, Mr Stalin, for agreeing to see me. I was in the United States recently. I had a long conversation with President Roosevelt and tried to ascertain what his leading ideas were. Now I have come to ask you what you are doing to change the world …

Stalin: Not so very much.

Wells: I wander around the world as a common man and, as a common man, observe what is going on around me.

Stalin: Important public men like yourself are not 'common men'. Of course, history alone can show how important this or that public man has been; at all events, you do not look at the world as a 'common man'.

Wells is not hugely impressed – he has already met Lenin in 1920 and warmed to him – and writes later in his autobiography: 'He [Stalin] has little of the quick uptake of President Roosevelt and none of the subtlety and tenacity of Lenin' – though he also says 'I have never met a man more candid, fair and honest.'

1992: On the morning of her death, the prolific writer Rosemary Sutcliff is still writing. The seventy-two-year-old author of *The Eagle of the Ninth* and *Sword at Sunset* is around two-thirds through the second draft of a book which has the provisional title *The Sword Song of Bjarni Sigurdson*. It becomes *Sword Song* when it is published five years later in 1997.

2009: Nigerian novelist Chimamanda Ngozi Adichie gives her TED Talk 'The Danger of a Single Story' at the Sheldonian Theatre in Oxford. She talks about the danger of single stories (especially in the media and literature, especially for the young) in creating stereotypes, and how she has forged her own voice. The recording of her twenty-minute talk on YouTube has more than twelve million views at time of going to press.

24

1901: Writer William Sydney Porter, better known as O. Henry, is released early from prison for good behaviour after serving three years for embezzlement, during which he has written and published more than a dozen stories (see 25 April).

25

1897: As gold fever strikes the country, twenty-one-year-old Jack London cuts short his studies at the University of California, Berkeley, and sets sail from San Francisco aboard a steamship to the Klondike in north-west Canada. As he writes in his 1913 autobiographical novel *John Barleycorn*: 'Yes, I had let career go hang, and was on the adventure-path again in quest of fortune.'

26

1602: Printer James Robertes enters 'A booke called the Revenge of Hamlett Prince Denmarke as yt was latelie Acted by the Lord Chamberleyne his servants' into the register of the Stationers' Company, the publishing trade guild whose monopoly on copyright later comes to an end with the 1710 Statute of Anne (see 10 April).

1915: In a public backing of the UK war effort, novelist Henry James gives up his American nationality and becomes a British citizen, writing to his friend the English poet Edmund Gosse, a sponsor for his application, 'Civis Britannicus sum!' He then sends out a press release via his agent James Brand Pinker, which is published in *The Times* explaining why he is doing this:

'Because of his having lived and worked in England for the best part of 40 years; because of his attachment to the country and his sympathy with it and its people; because of the long friendships and associations and interests he has formed here – including the acquisition of some property; all of which things have brought to a head his desire to throw his weight and personal allegiance, for whatever they may be worth, into the scale of the contending nation's present and future fortune.'

27

1937: Margaret Mitchell replies to a fan letter from a Mrs Blanche Maidwell in England. She writes that she is delighted to discover that there are fans of her book *Gone with the Wind*, published the previous

year, outside America but that she has no plans for a sequel. 'To tell the truth,' she admits, 'I do not know what happened to this obstinate couple after the end of the book.'

1986: Anthony Powell notes in his journal that his phone stalker has been in touch again. 'The imbecile rings from time to time, saying what a fan he is.' He rings at 6 a.m. and 8.30 a.m. Powell suggests a letter might be a better way of getting in touch. He rings again later. Powell suggests he might want to contact a psychiatrist. The caller says he has. Powell suggests that he contacts him again.

28

1814: At 4.15 a.m., twenty-one-year-old poet Percy Bysshe Shelley elopes with the sixteen-year-old future author of *Frankenstein*, Mary Wollstonecraft Godwin, travelling from London to Paris and leaving behind his pregnant wife. They are accompanied by Mary's stepsister, Jane. Here is how Shelley writes about the crossing in his 1817 travelogue *History of a Six Weeks' Tour*:

'The evening was most beautiful; there was but little wind, and the sails flapped in the flagging breeze: the moon rose, and night came on, and with the night a slow, heavy swell, and a fresh breeze, which soon produced a sea so violent as to toss the boat very much. I was dreadfully sea-sick, and as is usually my custom when thus affected, I slept during the greater part of the night, awaking only from time to time to ask where we were, and to receive the dismal answer each time – "Not quite half way."'

29

1835: Charlotte Brontë starts work as a teacher at Miss Wooler's school near Mirfield in West Yorkshire, where she has been a pupil (first day 17 January 1831). She leaves three years later, not having enjoyed the experience.

30

1935: Penguin, founded by Allen Lane following his failure to find anything cheap and decent to read at Exeter railway station, publishes the first mass-market paperback books. Initially they are colour-coded – green for crime, orange for fiction, blue for biography – and each of the first ten issued sells for sixpence. These are *Ariel* by André Maurois; *A Farewell to Arms* by Ernest Hemingway; *Poet's Pub* by Eric Linklater; *Madame Claire* by Susan Ertz; *The Unpleasantness at the Bellona Club* by Dorothy L. Sayers; *The Mysterious Affair at Styles* by Agatha Christie; *Twenty-Five* by Beverley Nichols; *William* by E. H. Young; *Gone to Earth* by Mary Webb; and *Carnival* by Compton Mackenzie.

31

1703: Daniel Defoe, author of *Robinson Crusoe*, is found guilty of seditious libel and sentenced to three days in the pillory for writing a pamphlet called 'The Shortest Way with the Dissenters'. This satirically suggests papists and nonconformists should be put to death. An urban legend has grown up that instead of lobbing dodgy fruit and vegetables at the poor man, the public merely tosses flowers.

1952: Evelyn Waugh writes to his friend Nancy Mitford about his forthcoming book *Men at Arms* that he has reread it and finds it 'awfully bad', adding though that 'there is no competition'.

1980: Harry Potter is born.

FINAL WORDS

'Don't let the awkward squad fire over my head'
Robert Burns (21 July 1796)

'It's a long time since I drank champagne'
Anton Chekhov (15 July 1904)

'You are wonderful'
Sir Arthur Conan Doyle (7 July 1930), to his wife

'What is the answer? ...
In that case, what is the question?'
Gertrude Stein (19 July 1946)

'A certain butterfly is already on the wing'
Vladimir Nabokov (2 July 1977)

AUGUST

When August days are hot an' dry,
I won't sit by an' sigh or die,
I'll get my bottle (on the sly)
And go ahead, and fish, and lie!
'In August' (1913) by Paul Laurence Dunbar

Births
Georgette Heyer (16 August 1902)
John Betjeman (28 August 1906)
Julio Cortázar (26 August 1914)
Garrison Keillor (7 August 1942)
Jeanette Winterson (27 August 1959)

Deaths
Honoré de Balzac (18 August 1850)
Naguib Mahfouz (30 August 2006)
Nina Bawden (22 August 2012)
Toni Morrison (5 August 2019)
Raymond Briggs (9 August 2022)

First published/performed
27 August 1955: *The Guinness Book of Records*
18 August 1958: *Lolita* by Vladimir Nabokov
12 August 1960: *Green Eggs and Ham* by Dr Seuss
1 August 1965: *Dune* by Frank Herbert
28 August 2018: *Normal People* by Sally Rooney

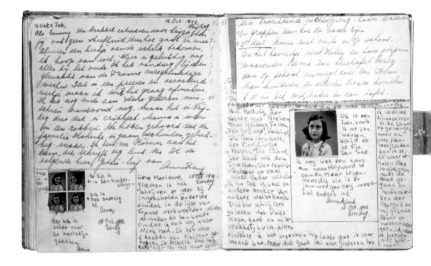

1

1944: Anne Frank makes the last entry in her diary. Three days later, acting on an anonymous tip-off, German police discover the attic where Anne, her family and four others have been hiding. They arrest and imprison them, then deport them on 3 September. Anne dies in Bergen-Belsen concentration camp in February or March the following year.

2

1869: Marian Evans, writing as George Eliot, begins work on *Middlemarch*. Despite finishing the first chapter by 5 August, she loses confidence the following month. But after a stop-start writing proccess, *Middlemarch* is published two years later (see 1 January).

3

1939: Biographer and novelist Winifred Peck – sister of *Punch* magazine editor Edmund Knox and aunt of novelist Penelope Fitzgerald – is beginning to believe that Faber & Faber has accepted her latest novel (one of what she calls 'my mild Anglican books') to offset the financial and social fallout from the publishing house losing a libel case. This involves a vicar in rural Oxfordshire mentioned in philosopher C. E. M. Joad's recent book *Guide to Modern Wickedness*, which Faber has just published.

4

1835: Another biographer and novelist, Elizabeth Gaskell, has been making notes on her experience of becoming a mother since March. But understandably it has not been easy to keep it up. This is what she writes on this day:

'It seems a very long time since I have written anything about my little darling, and I feel as if I had been negligent about it, only it is so difficult to know when to begin or when to stop when talking thinking or writing about her ... I fancy she says Mama, but I think it is only fancy ... How all of a woman's life, at least so it seems to me now, ought to have a reference to the period when she will be fulfilling one of her greatest & highest duties, those of a mother. I feel myself so unknowing, so doubtful about many things in her intellectual & moral treatment already, and what shall I be when she grows older, & asks those puzzling questions that children do? I hope I shall always preserve my present good intentions & sense of my holy trust, and then I must pray, to be forgiven for my errors, & led into a better course.'

5

1850: At a picnic, Herman Melville, who is currently in the middle of writing *Moby-Dick*, meets novelist Nathaniel Hawthorne, who has published *The Scarlet Letter* earlier in the year. They immediately hit it off as they trek up Monument Mountain in western Massachusetts, so much so that Melville dedicates his masterpiece to Hawthorne when it is published the following year (18 October in the UK, 14 November in the US).

6

1786: On 11 June the Mauchline kirk session records that 'The session being informed that Jean Armour is with child order their officer to summon her to attend upon sabbath first.' The father is twenty-seven-year-old Scottish poet Robert Burns, who pleads guilty to 'ante-nuptial fornication' with Jean, the woman who will soon become his wife. On this day, the kirk minutes state that: 'Robert Burns, John Smith, Mary Lindsay, Jean Armour and Agnes Auld appeared before the Congregation professing their repentance for the sin of fornication and they having each appeared two several sabbaths formerly were this day rebuked and absolved from the scandal.'

7

1873: Vincent van Gogh is delighted by his discovery of the poetry of Keats. He writes from his home in London to his friends Willem van Stockum and Caroline van Stockum-Haanebeek that the English poet is much less well known in Holland. 'He is adored by the painters here,' he says, 'and that is how I started reading him.' He recommends 'The Eve of St Agnes' as an example, but says it is too long to copy out in the letter.

8

1738: Jonathan Swift is down in the dumps, and perhaps a little paranoid about his letters being intercepted, as he explains to his lifelong friend the poet and satirist Alexander Pope in a letter:

'I desire you will look upon me as a man worn with years, and sunk by publick as well as personal vexations. I have entirely lost my memory, uncapable of conversation by a cruel deafness, which has lasted almost a year, and I despair of any cure. I say not this to increase your compassion (of which you have already too great a part) but as an excuse for my not being regular in my letters to you, and some few other friends. I have an ill name in the post office of both kingdoms, which makes the letters addressed to me not seldom miscarry, or be opened and read, and then sealed in a bungling manner before they come to my hands.'

9

1661: John Evelyn is introduced to the delights of pineapples, noting in his famous diary that I 'first saw the Queene-Pine brought from Barbados presented to his Majestie … the first that were ever seen in England were those sent to Cromwell foure years since'. Sadly, he has to wait seven more years, until 19 August 1668, before he actually gets to taste one at a dinner for the French ambassador:

'Standing by his Majesty at dinner in the presence, there was of that rare fruit called the king-pine growing in Barbadoes and the West Indies, the first of them I had ever seen. His Majesty having cut it up, was pleased to give me a piece off his own plate to taste of; but, in my opinion, it falls short of those ravishing varieties of deliciousness described in Captain Ligon's history, and others; but possibly it might, or certainly was, much impaired in coming so far; it has yet a grateful acidity, but tastes more like the quince and melon than of any other fruit he mentions.'

1854: It's publication day for Henry David Thoreau's *Walden; or, Life in the Woods*. Thoreau plays it cool in his diary ('To Boston. *Walden* published. Elder-berries. Waxwork yellowing'), but his friend the writer Ralph Waldo Emerson says that in the run-up to the big day he has noticed a 'tremble of great expectation' in Thoreau. Although this might also be because his previous book *A Week on the Concord and Merrimack Rivers* (1849) has not yet sold 300 copies.

10

1937: Writers Ernest Hemingway and Max Eastman unexpectedly bump into each other in the office of their editor Max Perkins at Scribner's publishing house in New York. Hemingway takes offence to Eastman's review of his recent *Death in the Afternoon*, in which he labelled Hemingway as an example of the 'False Hair on the Chest School of Writing'. Hemingway says to him: 'What do you mean accusing me of impotence?' then removes his shirt to show his chest hair, before unbuttoning Eastman's shirt to reveal a completely smooth chest. He then whacks Eastman on the nose with a book and wrestles him to the ground. Nobody is seriously hurt in the ensuing scuffle.

1821: There are plenty of high-jinks at Lord Byron's home in Ravenna, where Percy Shelley is visiting, as he explains in a letter to the English novelist Thomas Love Peacock:

'Lord Byron gets up at two. I get up, quite contrary to my usual custom, but one must sleep or die, like Southey's sea-snake at Kehama, at 12. After breakfast we sit talking till six. From six to eight we gallop through the pine forest which divides Ravenna from the sea; we then come home and dine, and sit up gossiping till six in the morning. I don't suppose this will kill me in a week or fortnight, but I shall not try it longer. Lord B.'s establishment consists, besides servants, of ten horses, eight enormous dogs, three monkeys, five

Publish'd Decem 1745   67   Pavo̶ bicolcaratus.

Camellia Japonica *Linn.*

cats, an eagle, a crow, and a falcon; and all these, except the horses, walk about the house, which every now and then resounds with their unarbitrated quarrels, as if they were the masters of it.

After I have sealed my letter, I find that my enumeration of the animals in this Circean Palace was defective, and that in a material point, I have just met on the grand staircase five peacocks, two guinea hens, and an Egyptian crane. I wonder who all these animals were before they were changed into these shapes.'

11

2018: On his deathbed, writer V. S. Naipaul asks magazine and newspaper editor Geordie Greig to read him 'Crossing the Bar' by Alfred, Lord Tennyson:

Sunset and evening star,
And one clear call for me!
And may there be no moaning of the bar,
When I put out to sea,

But such a tide as moving seems asleep,
Too full for sound and foam,
When that which drew from out
the boundless deep
Turns again home.

Twilight and evening bell,
And after that the dark!
And may there be no sadness of
farewell,
When I embark;

For tho' from out our bourne of
Time and Place
The flood may bear me far,
I hope to see my Pilot face to face
When I have cross'd the bar.

12

1975: Exactly twenty years after his death near Zurich and according to his wishes, four large packages containing Thomas Mann's never-before-seen diaries are officially unsealed. Inside are thirty-two notebooks filled with Mann's entries from 1918 to 1921 and then from 1933 to 1955. Over the intervening two decades there has been considerable speculation about what they might contain. They reveal his struggles to come to terms with his largely hidden homosexuality.

13

1955: This is the day on which historian David Kynaston believes Philip Larkin takes the train from Hull to London that inspires perhaps his most famous poem, 'The Whitsun Weddings'. It has been generally believed he travelled at Whitsun, but a train strike that weekend would have prevented him from doing so.

14

1040: Macbeth kills Duncan I in the Battle of Pitgaveny or Bothnagowan and takes the crown of Scotland.

15

1947: On the stroke of India's independence, Saleem Sinai is born (with telepathic powers) in *Midnight's Children* by Salman Rushdie.

16

1840: Actor William Macready (see 10 May) – the dedicatee of *Nicholas Nickleby* (1839) – goes for, and then describes in his diary, an eventful dinner at the house of his friend Charles Dickens:

'[I] was witness to a most painful scene after dinner. Forster [John Forster, Dickens's literary adviser and biographer], Maclise and myself were the guests. Forster got on to one of his headlong streams of talk (which he thinks argument) and waxed warm, and at last some sharp observations led to personal retorts between him and Dickens. He displayed his usual want of tact, and Dickens flew into so violent a passion as quite to forget himself and give Forster to understand that he was in his house, which he should be glad if he would leave. Forster behaved very foolishly. I stopped him; spoke to both of them and observed that for an angry instant they were about to destroy a friendship valuable to both. I drew from Dickens the admission that he had spoken in passion and would not have said what he said, could he have reflected; but he added he could not answer for his temper under Forster's provocations, and that he should do just the same again. Forster behaved very weakly; would not accept the repeated acknowledgment communicated to him that Dickens regretted the passion, etc., but stayed, skimbling-skambling a parcel of unmeaning words, and at last finding he could obtain no more, made a sort of speech, accepting what he had before declined. He was silent and not recovered no wonder! during the whole evening. Mrs Dickens had gone out in tears. It was a very painful scene.'

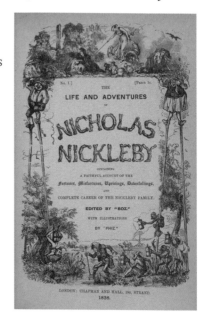

17

1936: A press release from Macmillan issued on this day contains some remarkable figures concerning the recent smash hit *Gone with the Wind*:

'The sales department of The Macmillan Company is mathematically minded. It has figured out some interesting facts about *Gone with the Wind*, the best seller by Margaret Mitchell. It appears that if all the copies of *Gone with the Wind* that have been printed were piled on top of each other the stack would be 50 times as high as the Empire State Building in New York City. Or if the pages of all these copies were laid end to end they would encircle the world at the Equator two and two-thirds times.

Some forty-five tons of boards and 34,000 yards of cloth have been used in the physical make-up of these books, and the paper already used would fill 24 carloads. Two printing plants are working on the book in three eight-hour shifts, and two binderies are fastening the sheets together.'

18

1799: From *Adam Bede* by George Eliot:

'The eighteenth of August was one of these days when the sunshine looked brighter in all eyes for the gloom that went before. Grand masses of cloud were hurried across the blue, and the great round hills behind the Chase seemed alive with their flying shadows; the sun was hidden for a moment, and then shone out warm again like a recovered joy; the leaves, still green, were tossed off the hedgerow trees by the wind; around the farmhouses there was a sound of clapping doors; the apples fell in the orchards; and the stray horses on the green sides of the lanes and on the common had their manes blown about their faces.'

1940: There's a direct bomb hit on one of the world's most literary residences, Lamb House in Rye. The garden room in which novelists Henry James and E. F. Benson, author of the *Mapp and Lucia* series, used to write (not at the same time) is destroyed in a lunchtime bombing raid. Over the years the house is also home to novelist Rumer Godden, essayist and poet A. C. Benson, publisher and illustrator Sir Brian Batsford and literary agent Graham Watson. Joan Aiken's novel *The Haunting of Lamb House* is a triptych of short stories about the building's ghosts during James and E. F. Benson's residencies.

THE STORY OF
LAMB HOUSE
RYE
The Home of Henry James
by
H. Montgomery Hyde

Price 7s. 6d.

1936: Gay Spanish playwright Federico García Lorca, having finished his play *La casa de Bernarda Alba* on 19 June, is arrested by a nationalist militia as part of its homophobic programme of 'social cleansing'. He is never seen again and his body is never found.

2013: A currently unnamed road in Portsmouth becomes the Ocean at the End of the Lane in recognition of Neil Gaiman's book of the same name. Gaiman grew up near the city, in Portchester and Southsea, and the local landscape inspires much of the book's setting. Summing up his reaction, Gaiman says he is: 'Gobsmacked, befuddled, delighted and baffled. When you make things up, you never expect them to creep out into the real world.'

19

1886: Joseph Conrad – born in Berdychiv, Ukraine, to a Polish family, but technically a Russian subject – offically becomes a British citizen. Novelist and navy officer Commodore Sir David Bone recalls Conrad telling him: 'I am more British than you are. You are only British because you could not help it.'

20

1945: Patrick O'Brian, author of the Aubrey–Maturin series of naval novels, officially changes his name from Patrick Russ.

21

1921: As a first birthday present, Christopher Robin Milne receives a teddy bear bought from Harrods by his father A. A. Milne. He will later call it Edward. 'Edward' is the textual inspiration for Winnie-the-Pooh, while an Eeyore toy is a Christmas present later this year. Illustrator E. H. Shepard does not use 'Edward', an Alpha model made by soft toy manufacturer J. K. Farnell, as a model for his famous illustrations of the Christopher Robin stories. Instead he picks his own son Graham's teddy, called Growler.

22

1913: Two years after the first building work begins in April 1911, Jack London's brand new twenty-six-room home, christened Wolf House, burns down just as he is about to move in. Designed by London and his wife Charmian, the house's features included nine fireplaces, a personal library, a two-storied living room, a built-in vacuum cleaning system and a wine cellar. A month before what he calls his 'castle' goes up in flames, probably as the result of oily rags spontaneously combusting, he writes: 'I am building my dream-house on my dream-ranch. My house will be standing, act of God permitting, for a thousand years.' Although the interior is entirely gutted, the moss-covered stone ruins of the building are still viewable today in the Jack London State Historic Park in California.

23

1939: Oxford undergraduate Iris Murdoch is hugely enjoying a fortnight's tour of the Cotswolds with student theatre company the Magpies. On this evening, performing a mixture of songs and play excerpts, she confides to her diary that 'Well, we did put on a show– but only just' – not all the actors have learnt their lines, costumes and scenery are unfinished, and the whole thing is under-rehearsed.

24

2009: US President Barack Obama releases his first summer holiday reading list:

Hot, Flat, and Crowded by Thomas Friedman
Plainsong by Kent Haruf
John Adams by David McCullough
The Way Home by George Pelecanos
Lush Life by Richard Price

25

1885: Wearing a black cashmere dress (changed to sage green for the television series), Laura Ingalls marries Almanzo Wilder in De Smet, South Dakota, the setting for several of the books in her *Little House* series. She omits saying 'obey' during the vows. Here's how the *De Smet Leader* newspaper reports it four days later: 'At the residence of the officiating clergyman, Rev. E. Brown, August 25, 1885. Mr Almanzo J. Wilder and Miss Laura

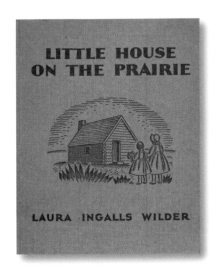

Ingalls, both of De Smet. Thus two more of our respected young people have united in the journey of life. May their voyage be pleasant, their joys be many and their sorrows few.'

26

1868: 'Proof of whole book came. It reads better than I expected. Not a bit sensational, but simple and true, for we really lived most of it; and if it succeeds that will be the reason of it. Mr N. likes it better now and says some girls who have read the manuscript say it is 'splendid'! As it is for them, they are the best critics, so I should be satisfied.' – Louisa M. Alcott, journal entry, on receiving the proofs of *Little Women*.

27

1942: Patricia Highsmith notes in her diary that what she is most interested in is perversion.

28

1833: On a visit to England, thirty-year-old Ralph Waldo Emerson heads to the Lake District to meet sixty-three-year-old William Wordsworth at his home, Rydal Mount near Ambleside. They talk for several hours about America, education, faith, sin, civil war, newspapers, tax and, of course, books. Wordsworth says he believes Lucretius is a better poet than Virgil, then takes the opportunity to recite three of his own sonnets inspired by his recent visit to Fingal's Cave on the Isle of Staffa in Scotland.

29

1883: The world's first Carnegie Library, the Dunfermline Carnegie Library, opens, part of the project funded by Scottish-American businessman and philanthropist Andrew Carnegie.

1962: Poet Robert Frost embarks on a goodwill tour to the Soviet Union, aiming to help ease the tensions of the Cold War. He meets Premier Nikita Khrushchev and pronounces him 'no fathead'.

30

1889: Oscar Wilde and Arthur Conan Doyle sit down to what becomes a hugely productive dinner at the Langham Hotel in London. Doyle is impressed with Wilde, writing in his autobiography that: 'His conversation left an indelible impression upon my mind. He towered above us all, and yet had the art of seeming to be interested in all that we could say.' Their dinner partner is Joseph Stoddart, the US editor of *Lippincott's Monthly Magazine*, who during the meal commissions each of them to write a story for him. Doyle's is 'The Sign of the Four', the second Sherlock Holmes story, which properly establishes the ongoing adventures of the consulting detective. Wilde's is 'The Picture of Dorian Gray', which provokes immediate and equal measures of success and scandal. A plaque celebrating the occasion is unveiled outside the Langham on 19 March 2010, by writer and broadcaster Gyles Brandreth.

2015: Keen that his unpublished works remain so after his death earlier in the year, around ten of Terry Pratchett's novels in progress are entirely destroyed when,

IN THE BEGINNING

GOD CREATED THE HEAVEN AND THE EARTH. ⟨AND
THE EARTH WAS WITHOUT FORM, AND VOID; AND
DARKNESS WAS UPON THE FACE OF THE DEEP, & THE
SPIRIT OF GOD MOVED UPON THE FACE OF THE WATERS.
⟨And God said, Let there be light: & there was light. And God saw the light,
that it was good: & God divided the light from the darkness. And God called
the light Day, and the darkness he called Night. And the evening and the
morning were the first day. ⟨And God said, Let there be a firmament in the
midst of the waters, & let it divide the waters from the waters. And God made
the firmament, and divided the waters which were under the firmament from
the waters which were above the firmament: & it was so. And God called the

according to his own instructions to be implemented after his passing,
they are smashed up by a steamroller and a concrete crusher at the
Great Dorset Steam Fair in England. The remains of the hard drive
go on show in the local Salisbury Museum.

31

1916: English bookbinder and publisher Thomas Cobden-Sanderson
begins to destroy the remarkable Doves typeface which he has
devised and used with partner Emery Walker over the last fifteen
years to publish lavish editions including a *Paradise Lost* and a Bible.
Sadly, by this point their working relationship has utterly collapsed,
and to ensure there is no further discussion about ownership of the
typeface, Cobden-Sanderson starts throwing all 500,000 pieces of
the sixteen-point type in the River Thames in London on this night.
He finishes by January the following year. Happily, it is partially
retrieved over the years and is used by Lara Maiklem in her 2019
book *Mudlarking* for the book title on the front cover, the running
heads at the top of each page, the epigraphs and the first letter of
every chapter.

1931: Karen Blixen/Isak Dinesen, author of *Out of Africa* and *Babette's
Feast*, arrives back in Denmark from her life in Africa and never returns.

FINAL WORDS

'Take me, for I come to Thee'
John Bunyan (31 August 1688)

'I am sorry to trouble you chaps. I don't know how you get along so fast with the traffic on the road these days'
Ian Fleming (12 August 1964), to the ambulance
staff driving him to hospital

'Mama'
Truman Capote (25 August 1984)

'Go away. I'm alright.'
H. G. Wells (13 August 1946)

'No. Awfully jolly of you to suggest it, though.'
Ronald Knox (24 August 1957) to Lady Elton asking if she
should read his translation of the New Testament to him

SEPTEMBER

Lyric night of the lingering Indian Summer,
Shadowy fields that are scentless but full of singing,
Never a bird, but the passionless chant of insects,
Ceaseless, insistent.
'September Midnight' (1914) by Sara Teasdale

Births
James Hilton (9 September 1900)
Cesare Pavese (9 September 1908)
William Golding (19 September 1911)
Julia Donaldson (16 September 1948)
George R. R. Martin (20 September 1948)

Deaths
William Hazlitt (18 September 1830)
Françoise Sagan (24 September 2004)
Helen Cresswell (26 September 2005)
David Foster Wallace (12 September 2008)
Hilary Mantel (22 September 2022)

First published/performed
3 September 1899: *Three Men in a Boat (To Say Nothing of the Dog)*
by Jerome K. Jerome
21 September 1937: *The Hobbit, or There and Back Again* by
J. R. R. Tolkien
14 September 1946: *Thomas the Tank Engine* by the Rev W. Awdry
17 September 1954: *Lord of the Flies* by William Golding
8 September 1961: *Perry Rhodan* by K. H. Scheer and Walter Ernsting

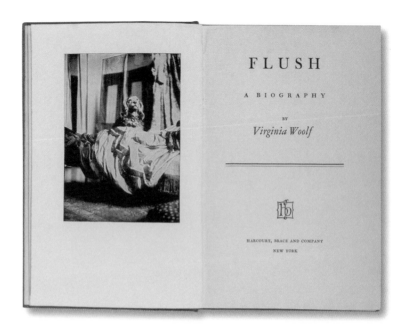

1

1846: Elizabeth Barrett Browning's cocker spaniel Flush is dognapped as she steps into her carriage after a shopping trip. In fact she has been targeted by specialist dognappers since leaving home that morning, and it is the third time Flush has been taken by a dog-stealing organisation called the Fancy. Previously their representatives have even turned up at her home and demanded ransom money (paid both times). This time her husband Robert suggests not paying, but Elizabeth and a servant manage to find Flush by tracking down the wife of the dognapper to the Whitechapel area and appealing to her better nature. Elizabeth describes her as 'an immense feminine bandit'.

1865: Alfred, Lord Tennyson visits German writer Johann Wolfgang von Goethe's study, as Tennyson's son Hallam recounts in his 1897 biography of the English poet:

Went with Mr Marshall – secretary to the Grand Duchess – to Goethe's town-house. No key there for the rooms. The old woman said that she was alone in the house, and could not possibly go and fetch it.

A. was touched by seeing the "Salve" on the door-mat, and all Goethe's old boots at the entrance. Mr Marshall brought the Herr Direktor, for eight years Goethe's secretary, who courteously left his dinner to come. Mr Marshall expressed his regret that there was no time to write to Madame von Goethe for an order to see the study. The Director made no remark at the time, but, when he had shown us the busts and gems and statuettes, and Goethe's own drawings, he took us into the sacred study. One cannot explain in words the awe and sadness with which this low dark room filled A. The study is narrow, and in proportion long. In the middle was a table with a cushion on it where Goethe would lean his arms, and a chair with a cushion where he sometimes sat, but his habit was to pace up and down and dictate to his secretary. On one side of the room was a bookcase about two-thirds up the wall, with boxes for his manuscripts. There were also visiting cards, strung like bills together, and Goethe's old, empty, wine bottles, in which the wine had left patterns like frost patterns. On the other side of the room was a calendar of things that had struck him in newspapers. Here a door opened to his bedroom. Such a melancholy little place! By the bed was an arm chair, to which at last he used to move from his bed for a little change. All round the wall, by the bed and the chair, a dark green leafy carpet or tapestry was fastened half-way up the wall of the room. On the washing-stand was some of the last medicine he took. The one window at the foot of the bed was partly boarded up. It looked I think into the garden.'

1995: Having been made redundant from his job with ITV, Lee Child goes shopping for pens and paper and sits down to write what will become the first Jack Reacher novel, published in 1997 as *Killing Floor*. He begins each new book in the series on the anniversary of this day.

2

1566: Terrible scenes at a performance attended in Oxford by Elizabeth I of the play *Palamon and Arcyte* by Richard Edwardes. When part of the staircase in Christ Church Hall collapses at the start of the play, three people are killed and five people injured, according to eyewitness Miles Windsor, an actor who records:

'which disaster coming to the Queen's knowledge, she sent forthwith the Vice-chancellor [actually her Lord Chamberlain, William Howard] and her Chirugeons to help them, and to have a care that they want nothing for their recovery.'

Remarkably, the show – the text of which has not survived to the present day – continues, and according to Windsor: 'Afterwards the Actors performed their parts so well, that the Queen laughed heartily thereat, and gave the Author of the Play great thanks for his pains.'

1914: Politician and man of letters Charles Masterman sets up the British War Propaganda Bureau to produce books, maps, cartoons and pamphlets to aid the war effort in general and encourage the US to enter the war on the British side in particular. He invites a who's who of the nation's leading male writers to a meeting on this day to discuss joining the bureau, including H. G. Wells, Thomas Hardy, Ford Madox Ford, John Masefield, Arthur Conan Doyle, G. K. Chesterton and Arnold Bennett. Rudyard Kipling apologises for his absence but offers his future help. George Bernard Shaw is not invited on the grounds of being unreliable. There is general enthusiasm, although Hardy refuses to officially take part, and Wells has mixed feelings. The work is kept admirably secret, and even after it is disbanded at the end of the war, the bureau's existence is not made public until 1935.

3

1802: 'Composed upon Westminster Bridge, September 3, 1802', by William Wordsworth:

Earth has not any thing to show more fair:
Dull would he be of soul who could pass by
A sight so touching in its majesty:
This City now doth, like a garment, wear
The beauty of the morning; silent, bare,
Ships, towers, domes, theatres, and temples lie
Open unto the fields, and to the sky;
All bright and glittering in the smokeless air.
Never did sun more beautifully steep
In his first splendour, valley, rock, or hill;
Ne'er saw I, never felt, a calm so deep!
The river glideth at his own sweet will:
Dear God! the very houses seem asleep;
And all that mighty heart is lying still!

Despite the title, Wordsworth probably writes most of this sonnet on 31 July 1802, when he enjoys this view of the capital, only finishing it on the date indicated. This is how his sister Dorothy writes of the scene in her journal on that day as the couple depart London, bound for Calais around 6 a.m.:

'It was a beautiful morning. The city, St Paul's, with the river, and a multitude of little boats, made a most beautiful sight as we crossed Westminster Bridge. The houses were not overhung by their cloud of smoke, and they were spread out endlessly, yet the sun shone so brightly, with such a fierce light; that there was something like the purity of one of nature's own grand spectacles.'

1869: Leo Tolstoy is travelling on business when he becomes inexplicably anxious. He and his servant stop for the night in a village called Arzamas, 250 miles east of Moscow. Tolstoy's spiritual unease worsens when he's shown into his room, a simple white-walled space with dark red furniture. He then endures a long dark night of the soul, convinced of the close presence of death, and generally seized with terror. Although this feeling will lessen in the morning, the general fear of his demise haunts him for the rest of his life. On the good side, he manages to channel his feelings into his successful novella *The Death of Ivan Ilyich*.

4

1893: Twenty-seven-year-old Beatrix Potter writes a picture letter to five-year-old Noel Moore, the son of her former governess Annie Carter, who is ill in bed with scarlet fever in London. It marks the first appearance of Peter Rabbit. 'I don't know what to write to you,' she says, 'so I shall tell you a story about four little rabbits whose names were Flopsy, Mopsy, Cottontail and Peter.'

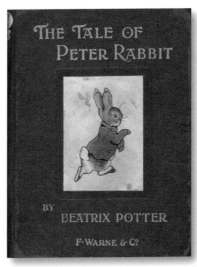

5

2008: The Diagram Prize for Oddest Title of the Year has been doing what it says on the tin since 1978; a special 'Diagram of Diagrams' prize is announced today. It goes to the 1996 winner, *Greek Rural Postmen and Their Cancellation Numbers*, edited by Derek Willan, published by the Hellenic Philatelic Society of Great Britain.

6

1642: The new Puritan government closes theatres in London. They remain shut for eighteen years.

1890: When the captain of the *Roi des Belges* falls ill, thirty-two-year-old Joseph Conrad temporarily takes his place as the skipper in the small boat travelling down the Congo River from the Stanley Falls to Leopoldville (now Kinshasa). On board is Georges Klein, the company agent of the Belgian trading company that owns the boat, who is suffering badly from dysentery, from which he will die on 21 September. Although the trip goes largely as planned, it provides Conrad with inspiration for his novella *The Heart of Darkness* – the harmless Klein becoming the more problematic Kurtz – which is published nine years later.

2022: While travelling on London's Tube network, writer Lemn Sissay notices his work 'Dei Miracole' on display as part of the Poems on the Underground series, originally launched in 1986. He takes out a Sharpie pen and signs it. Nobody on the crowded commuter carriage appears to notice. 'I signed my own poem,' he tweets, 'then took a selfie, to absolutely no reaction from the people in the carriage. London.'

7

1911: Poet Wilhelm Apollinaris de Kostrowitzky, better known as Guillaume Apollinaire, is arrested on suspicion of stealing the *Mona*

Lisa (and several Egyptian statuettes) from the Louvre in Paris on 21 August. He is imprisoned for six days in the city's Santé prison, where he writes one of his finest poems, 'A la Santé', before being released without charge.

8

1786: Travelling to Italy, Johann Wolfgang von Goethe arrives in Innsbruck at 11 a.m. and lunches at the Goldener Adler inn. Here he notices the son of the landlord, whom he describes as the spitting image of 'Söller', a character from his work *Die Mitschuldigen* (*The Accomplices*). 'I'm gradually coming across the characters I've invented,' he notes in his diary. The Goldener Adler, established 1390, is still in business today and an oil painting marking the meeting hangs on its walls.

9

1902: P. G. Wodehouse takes the plunge and leaves his position at the Hong Kong and Shanghai Bank to try his luck as a writer. His first novel is published on 18 September, *The Pothunters*, which has been partly serialised in the *Public School Magazine* earlier in the year.

1910: Alice B. Toklas moves into Gertrude Stein's flat at 27 rue de Fleurus on the Left Bank in Paris on a permanent basis, having met Stein for the first time on 8 September 1907. Over the years, they turn the apartment into an impressive literary and avant-garde salon.

1953: Flann O'Brien/Brian O'Nolan/Myles na Gopaleen writes to Underwood complaining about his previously trusty typewriter. He reports that after phoning in a problem about his ribbon no longer moving, an operative from the Dublin branch has visited his home and spent quarter of an hour fixing the issue. But despite being asked to generally give the machine a good wash and brush up, it appears this has not been done, on top of which, it has now developed a lower-/uppercase misalignment problem and is turning double spaces into treble spaces. O'Brien says he has now fixed these problems himself but was enraged this morning to receive two bills from Underwood for the work involved, which he refuses to pay. Today the typewriter is held by the John J. Burns Library at Boston College in the US.

10

1923: John Reith, general manager of what was known at that time as the British Broadcasting Company, has a eureka moment. 'Everything is now in shape for the BBC magazine,' he writes in his diary, 'and from various alternatives I chose *Radio Times* for the title.'

1950: The ninety-four-year-old George Bernard Shaw loses his balance while pruning fruit trees at his home in Hertfordshire, falls, and fractures his thigh. He is taken to hospital with, according to press reports, a small library of books.

11

1892: Ten-year-old Virginia Stephen and her family enjoy a boat excursion to Godrevy lighthouse while holidaying in Cornwall, and she signs the visitors' book. She visits again on 17 September 1894, although this time her father signs her name for her. These trips, and similar ones during her childhood to the same area, partly inspire her novel *To the Lighthouse* (1927). The visitors' book is sold for £10,250 when it comes up for auction at Bonhams on 22 November 2011.

201

1947: Andy Dufresne's wife Linda and her lover are murdered in Stephen King's 1982 novella *Rita Hayworth and Shawshank Redemption*. Andy is found guilty of the crime and incarcerated in Shawshank Prison, from where he makes his dramatic escape on 12 March 1975.

2022: Spanish writer Javier Marías dies in Madrid, which means the Throne of Redonda becomes vacant (see 17 February).

12

1846: Poet Elizabeth Barrett elopes with poet Robert Browning, marrying in secret (see 20 May).

13

1986: Two young women in a red VW pinch Evelyn Couch's parking spot in *Fried Green Tomatoes at the Whistle Stop Café* by Fannie Flagg. They laughingly tell her they are 'younger and faster' before wandering off to do some grocery shopping. They return to find an

incandescent Evelyn smashing into their car, explaining: 'I'm older than you are and have more insurance than you do.'

14

1814: Lawyer Francis Scott Key is an eyewitness to the attack on Fort McHenry in Maryland by British armed forces. The American troops resist the attack and Key is particularly struck by a large American flag (fifteen stars and fifteen stripes) flying over the fort in celebration. Inspired, he begins a poem known initially as 'Defence of Fort McHenry' but later as the lyrics for 'The Star-Spangled Banner', the first verse of which runs:

O say can you see, by the dawn's early light,
What so proudly we hailed at the twilight's last gleaming,
Whose broad stripes and bright stars through the perilous fight,
O'er the ramparts we watched, were so gallantly streaming?
And the rocket's red glare, the bombs bursting in air,
Gave proof through the night that our flag was still there;

O say does that star-spangled banner yet wave
O'er the land of the free and the home of the brave?

15

1507: Walter Chepman, a merchant, and Androw Myllar, probably a printer-bookseller, are delighted to be granted a royal charter by King James IV to establish the first printing press in Scotland in order to print Scottish laws and acts of Parliament as well as historical and liturgical texts. They import a press from France and set their monopoly up in Cowgate, Edinburgh.

2003: Stephen King wins the prestigious National Book Foundation's Medal for Distinguished Contribution to American Letters, the board of directors acknowledging that: 'He has earned the reputation among readers and booklovers as a genre-defying stylist, vivid storyteller, and master of suspense.' Previous winners include Saul Bellow, Eudora Welty, Toni Morrison, Studs Terkel, John Updike, Ray Bradbury, Arthur Miller and Philip Roth. In his acceptance speech on 19 November, King says that he acknowledges some people believe he is just a 'rich hack' and undeserving of the award, but that he hopes that this is a turning point in the acceptance of popular writers rather than mere tokenism.

16

1939: Rusty Regan disappears in *The Big Sleep* by Raymond Chandler; four days later his car is discovered in a garage. His whereabouts are crucial to the unravelling of the case, which is investigated by Philip Marlowe.

17

1996: Oprah Winfrey launches a television book club on her daytime television show. The first choice is *The Deep End of the Ocean* by Jacquelyn Mitchard. It has been selling quite well, especially for a first novel, but the Oprah effect propels it to the top of the bestseller lists and it is later turned into a film starring Michelle Pfeiffer.

18

1849: Writing from Norfolk, Virginia, to his aunt and mother-in-law Maria Clemm (whom he calls 'Muddy'), Edgar Allan Poe is in a buoyant mood. He talks about his latest lecture tours in the area, his finances and his approaching marriage (following the death two years earlier of his wife Virginia) to his childhood friend Sarah Elmira Royster Shelton. Sadly things do not go to plan ... (see 3 October).

19

1819: A walk by the River Itchen near Winchester inspires John Keats to write 'To Autumn', which starts 'Season of mists and mellow fruitfulness / Close bosom-friend of the maturing sun'.

On 22 September he writes to his friend John Hamilton Reynolds:

'How beautiful the season is now – How fine the air. A temperate sharpness about it. Really, without joking, chaste weather – Dian skies – I never liked stubble-fields so much as now – Aye better than the chilly green of the Spring. Somehow, a stubble-field looks warm – in the same way that some pictures look warm. This struck me so much in my Sunday's walk that I composed upon it.'

1973: Paul Theroux catches the 15.30 from London Victoria bound for Folkestone, then Paris and all points east across Europe and Asia as he gathers material for the travelogue that will become *The Great Railway Bazaar* (1975).

20

1592: Playboy playwright Robert Greene publishes a pamphlet called 'A Groats-Worth of Witte bought with a Million of Repentance', an unremarkable offering but for what appears to be the first published reference to William Shakespeare. It is not a positive one, as Greene warns his colleagues to be wary of an up-and-coming twentysomething actor-playwright:

'There is an upstart Crow, beautified with our feathers, that with his Tygers hart wrapt in a Players hyde supposes he is as well able to bombast out a blanke verse as the best of you: and beeing an absolute Johannes factotum is in his owne conceit the onely Shake-scene in a countrey.'

21

1599: Thomas Platter, a doctor and keen traveller from Basel, is visiting England as part of a tour of Europe and naturally keeping a diary of his

trip. Today he is in London and just after lunch, at about 2 p.m., he goes to see a performance of Shakespeare's *Julius Caesar* at the newly built Globe Theatre, which he calls 'the house with the thatched roof'. He describes the tragedy as 'excellent'.

22

1241: Icelandic poet, historian, chieftain and politician Snorri Sturluson is murdered in his home, probably at the behest of Haakon IV, King of Norway. He is best known today for writing the *Prose Edda* and *Heimskringla* and probably *Egil's Saga,* which have helped to preserve Norse myths. Several hundred years after the murder, J. R. R. Tolkien suggests that he would prefer his students at Oxford to read Snorri Sturluson than Shakespeare, and indeed most of the dwarves' names in *The Hobbit* (as well as 'Gandalf') appear in the *Prose Edda*.

1586: While leading English troops at the Battle of Zutphen, poet, courtier, soldier and all-round Renaissance man Sir Philip Sidney is wounded in the left thigh with a musket ball, so seriously in fact that he dies of his injuries on 17 October. Sidney's friend and biographer Fulke Greville recounts that he might have survived, but selflessly lent his thigh armour to his comrade-in-arms Sir William Pelham, who had none. Greville adds that after the battle, on returning back to camp, 'being thirstie with excess of bleeding, he called for drink, which was presently brought him; but as he was putting the bottle to his mouth, he saw a poor Souldier carryed along, who had eaten his last at the same Feast, gastly casting up his eyes at the bottle. Which Sir Philip perceiving, took it from his head, before he drank, and delivered it to the poor man, with these words, "Thy necessity is greater than mine."'

1598: Playwright Ben Jonson kills actor Gabriel Spenser in a duel in Hoxton, London, despite Jonson claiming Spenser has fought with a longer sword. He admits guilt in his trial at the Old Bailey, where the jury is told that he 'feloniosly and wilfully struck and beat the said Gabriel' while wielding 'a certain sword of iron and steel called a rapier, of the price of three shillings'. But the cunning Jonson pleads benefit of clergy and so escapes the death penalty by simply reading a passage from the Bible, submitting to branding on his thumb, forfeiting some property and accepting a short prison sentence.

1926: James Joyce and American novelist Thomas Wolfe are on the same sightseeing bus touring the battlefield at Waterloo. However,

Wolfe is too overawed to introduce himself so they do not meet.
He writes to his lover, Aline Bernstein, that Joyce realises he has been
spotted ('the great man himself taking an occasional crafty shot at me
with his good eye'), going on to say that:

'Joyce was very simple, very nice. He walked next to the old guide
who showed us around, listening with apparent interest to his
harangue delivered in broken English, and asking him questions.
We came home to Brussels through a magnificent forest, miles
in extent ... Joyce got a bit stagey on the way home, draping his
overcoat poetically around his shoulders ... the idea of Joyce and
me being at Waterloo at the same time, and aboard a sight-seeing
bus, struck me as insanely funny. I sat on the back seat making
idiot noises in my throat, and crooning all the way back through
the forest. I think they really might have been a little grand about
it if they had known they were discovered. But they were just like
common people out sight-seeing.'

23

1912: The literary journal *Poetry: A Magazine of Verse* is launched by poet Harriet Monroe. It becomes hugely influential and boasts not only an inclusive open-door policy but also a who's who of twentieth-century writers among its contributors, including T. S. Eliot, whose 'The Love Song of J. Alfred Prufrock' first appears in its pages in June 1915.

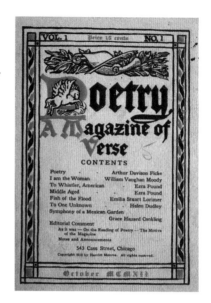

24

1891: Thirteen-year-old orphan John Masefield starts his first sea apprenticeship on HMS *Conway*, a naval training school. Among the books he reads on board are Robert Louis Stevenson's *Treasure Island*. He jumps ship four years later in New York, keen to become a writer.

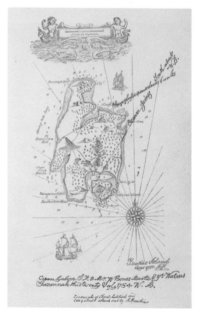

25

1973: It's the day of Chilean poet Pablo Neruda's funeral. An adviser to and supporter of President Salvador Allende, he is very much persona non grata among followers of Augusto Pinochet, who has taken charge following the military coup a few days earlier. Pinochet refuses a request for Neruda to receive a state funeral, but nevertheless thousands of people turn out to pay their tributes. They make clear their opposition to the new 'government' by singing the left-wing 'Internationale' anthem as the coffin is carried on foot through the city.

26

1997: A memorial statue to Dr Samuel Johnson's favourite pet cat, Hodge, is unveiled today by the Lord Mayor of London, Sir Roger Cook, outside Johnson's home at 17 Gough Square. Hodge sits on top of his master's dictionary with two oyster shells by his paws, an allusion to the snack his master used to bring him, while the inscription reads:

HODGE

'a very fine cat indeed'
belonging to SAMUEL JOHNSON (1709–1784)
of Gough Square.

'Sir, when a man is tired of London
he is tired of life: for there is in
London all that life can afford.'

'The chief glory of every people
arises from its authors.'

In Boswell's famous biography of Dr Samuel Johnson, he recalls one day when Hodge scrambles onto Johnson's lap. Boswell remarks that he is a fine cat. Johnson replies: 'Why yes, Sir, but I have had cats whom I liked better than this,' then hurriedly adds, in case this might upset Hodge: 'But he is a very fine cat, a very fine cat indeed.'

The bronze statue is the work of sculptor Jon Bickley, who used his own cat as a model.

27

1960: Novelist Christa Wolf is asked during a Russian newspaper interview to explain what she did on 27 September in as much detail as possible. Intrigued by such a detailed question, she begins a diary of all the rest of the September 27ths in her life until her death in 2011.

1962: The latest episode in CBS's television series *Perry Mason* airs tonight, *The Case of the Bogus Books*. It revolves around the theft from an antiquarian bookshop of a first edition of *The Life and Opinions of Tristram Shandy, Gentleman* by Laurence Sterne.

28

1930: Virginia Woolf plans to head to her writing lodge in her garden at Monk's House near Lewes, Sussex, as she explains in a letter to her friend Ethel Smyth:

'[I] shall smell a red rose; shall gently surge across the lawn (I move as if I carried a basket of eggs on my head) light a cigarette, take my writing board on my knee; and let myself down, like a diver, very cautiously into the last sentence I wrote yesterday.'

Her husband Leonard writes that Virgina heads to the lodge 'with the regularity of a stockbroker'.

29

1661: Samuel Pepys does not enjoy a new production of Shakespeare's *A Midsummer Night's Dream* on this afternoon. 'I had never seen

before nor shall ever again,' he complains, 'for it is the most insipid ridiculous play that ever I saw in my life'.

30

1659: Robinson Crusoe makes it to land after he has been shipwrecked in *Robinson Crusoe* (1719) by Daniel Defoe.

1934: Lieutenant-Colonel William Butler-Bowden announces the discovery in a letter to *The Times* of the only surviving manuscript of mystic Margery Kempe's 'Book', unearthed by accident during a game of table tennis at their home. He threatens to burn it on a bonfire as it is cluttering up the ping-pong cupboard and making it hard to track down bats and balls, but happily does no such thing.

FINAL WORDS

'Well this is a great comfort. I have followed you distinctly and I feel as if I was to be myself again'
Sir Walter Scott (21 September 1832) to his son-in-law who read to him from the Bible

'My friend, return to literature'
Ivan Turgenev (3 September 1883), to Leo Tolstoy

'I am dying old friend'
Wilkie Collins (23 September 1889),
a note to his friend and doctor Francis Carr Beard

'God bless Captain Vere'
Herman Melville (28 September 1891), referring to
one of the characters in his work *Billy Budd*

'I'm going to stop now, but I'm going to sharpen the axe before I put it up, dear'
E. E. Cummings (3 September 1962),
to his wife while chopping wood

JANE EYRE

BY CHARLOTTE BRONTË

GEORGE ROUTLEDGE AND SONS.

OCTOBER

And suns grow meek, and the meek suns grow brief,
And the year smiles as it draws near its death.
'October' (1866) by William Cullen Bryant

Births
R. K. Narayan (10 October 1906)
James Herriot/James Wight (3 October 1916)
Philip Pullman (19 October 1946)
Elfriede Jelinek (20 October 1946)
Zadie Smith (27 October 1975)

Deaths
Zane Grey (23 October 1939)
Brian Friel (2 October 2015)
Henning Mankell (5 October 2015)
Dario Fo (13 October 2016)
Anthea Bell (18 October 2018)

First published/performed
19 October 1847: *Jane Eyre* by Charlotte Brontë
14 October 1926: *Winnie-the-Pooh* by A. A. Milne
13 October 1930: *The Murder at the Vicarage* by Agatha Christie
16 October 1950: *The Lion, the Witch and the Wardrobe* by C. S. Lewis
29 October 1959: 'Astérix le Gaulois' (magazine serial) by René
Goscinny (text) and Albert Uderzo (illustrations)

1

1782: Diarist, historian and close friend of Samuel Johnson Hester Thrale spends the day worrying in her diary about whether she should marry again following the death of her wealthy husband, Henry Thrale. In the end she decides to take the leap with Italian singer and composer – and Roman Catholic – Gabriel Piozzi. They are married on 23 July 1784, a decision that scandalises polite society and sees Johnson and her own family cut off their friendship with her. The diary, known today as *Thraliana*, is not published until 1942.

1919: It's deadline day for Sergei Prokofiev to complete the score of his work *The Love for Three Oranges*. He finishes bang on 2 p.m.

2

1944: Dylan Thomas fails to attend the wedding in London of his close friend the Welsh poet Vernon Watkins, where he is supposed to

be best man. He claims he set off in good time in a taxi but forgets where it is taking place, and a drive around the capital searching for it proves fruitless. Remarkably, it does not ruin their friendship, although Gwen – the new Mrs Watkins – is not at all amused. She suggests he was simply too shy to turn up.

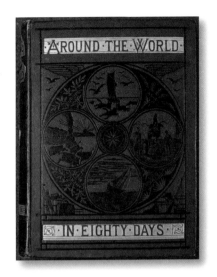

1872: At 8.45 p.m., Phileas Fogg leaves London in his bid to go *Around the World in 80 Days* by Jules Verne (see 21 December).

3

1800: Out for a walk in Grasmere near their home, William and Dorothy Wordsworth bump into an elderly gentleman gathering leeches. The meeting inspires William nearly two years later to write his poem 'Resolution and Independence', initially with the less stately name 'The Leech-Gatherer'. Here is one of the twenty stanzas:

He with a smile did then his words repeat;
And said that, gathering leeches, far and wide
He travelled; stirring thus about his feet
The waters of the pools where they abide.
'Once I could meet with them on every side;
But they have dwindled long by slow decay;
Yet still I persevere, and find them where I may.'

The poem is later parodied in *Alice's Adventures through the Looking-Glass* by Lewis Carroll (1871) in the White Knight's slightly confusingly titled poem 'Haddocks' Eyes'.

1822: Washington Irving is beavering away on a trip to Germany, as he explains in a letter written on this day to his sister:

'I am now scribbling late at night in a little village in the valley of Kenseg in the heart of the Black Forest. The inn is such an one as is sometimes shown on the stage, where benighted travellers arrive and meet with fearful adventures. We where shewn into a great public room, wainscotted with wood, blackened by smoke, in where were waggoners and rustic travellers supping and smoking; a huge, rambling staircase led up to a number of old-fashioned wainscotted apartments. The hostess is dressed in one of the antique costumes of the country, and we are waited upon by a servant man in a dress that would figure to advantage in a melodrama; and a servant maid that is a Patagonian in size, and looks, as to costume, as if she had come out of the ark.'

1849: Edgar Allan Poe is found wandering around Baltimore, semi-conscious, in a state of disorientation and wearing somebody else's clothes, 'a stained faded, old bombazine [silk] coat, pantaloons of a similar character, a pair of worn-out shoes run down at the heels, and an old straw hat'. He dies on 7 October, calling out the name 'Reynolds' several times the previous night for no apparent reason. Neither his death certificate nor medical records have survived, giving rise to various theories about the cause of his death, ranging from alcoholism and rabies to epilepsy, suicide or even perhaps as a result of being forced to take part in electoral fraud (see 19 January).

1867: Anthony Trollope resigns from his day job as a senior administrator at the Post Office, during which he has introduced pillar boxes to Britain, to become a full-time writer.

4

1937: Harriet Vane gives her husband-to-be Lord Peter Wimsey a John Donne manuscript page in *Busman's Honeymoon* (1937) by Dorothy L. Sayers. Wimsey explains that it is a letter from Donne to one of his parishioners about love, both human and divine.

1939: Welsh poets Lynette Roberts and Keidrych Rhys get married at Llansteffan, Wales. Dylan Thomas is the best man. This time he turns up (see 2 October), having borrowed his friend Vernon Watkins's brown suit for the day. Thomas writes to say thank you, mentioning that the occasion is notable for 'the beauty of the female attendants, the brown suit of the best man, the savage displeasure of Keidrych's mother' as well as Rhys looking rather miserable.

5

1902: An estimated 50,000 people turn out for the funeral of French novelist Émile Zola at Montmartre cemetery in Paris. Among them is Alfred Dreyfus, who famously received Zola's staunch public support when accused of treason some years earlier, and many miners who shout 'Germinal, Germinal' as his coffin passes, in tribute to Zola's masterpiece about a coal-mining strike in the north of France.

1949: New York-based writer Helene Hanff pens her first letter to London antiquarian bookshop Marks & Co. which is found at 84 Charing Cross Road, later the title of her epistolary memoir. She encloses a list of her 'most pressing problems', books which she'd like to buy that cost no more than $5 each.

6

1983: At 10 a.m., William Golding is phoned by a Swedish reporter who claims he has a 50/50 chance of being awarded the Nobel Prize in literature. Golding writes in his diary that he is very excited but tries hard to remain calm. It is confirmed by the media at just after 1 p.m. that he has indeed won. He goes riding to avoid the phone, which rings off the hook, but returns to find broadcast media on his doorstep. They all leave by 10 p.m.

7

1571: In the seas of western Greece, a feverish but battle-hungry Miguel de Cervantes is wounded at the Battle of Lepanto, fought between a coalition of Christian European navies and the navy of the Ottoman Empire. His chest wound is not too serious, but he loses his left hand, and while amputation as the result of the musket shots' damage is not required, his arm is effectively non-functioning for the rest of his life. It does not put him off a literary career, including his *El ingenioso hidalgo don Quixote de la Mancha* (1605–15).

1955: At about 11 p.m., Allen Ginsberg reads part of his iconic poem *Howl* in public for the first time at the Six Gallery in San Francisco. The only promotion is via a postcard produced by Ginsberg which promises: 'Remarkable collection of angels all gathered at once in the same spot. Wine, music, dancing girls, serious poetry, free satori. Small collection for wine and postcards. Charming event.' Other poets reciting that night include Gary Snyder, Philip Lamantia, Michael McClure, Philip Whalen and Kenneth Rexroth. In the audience are Lawrence Ferlinghetti, Neal Cassady and Jack Kerouac. Kerouac later describes in his *The Dharma Bums* (1958) organising a whip-round for wine and urging everybody to 'slug from the jug' while 'everybody was yelling "Go! Go! Go!" (like a jam session)'.

8

1862: Sophia Tolstoy confides to her diary that she has been feeling rotten since yesterday, when her husband Leo told her he doesn't trust her love.

9

1899: The forty-four-year-old Lyman Frank Baum finishes *The Emerald City*, later to be renamed *The Wizard of Oz*. He marks the moment by framing the little pencil he uses for the last section with a note of the date underneath it: 'With this pencil I wrote the manuscript for *The Emerald City*. L. Frank Baum.' He hangs it on the wall of his study.

1951: For the first time, castaways on BBC Radio's *Desert Island Discs* programme hosted by Roy Plomley are give a choice of book to take with them. The first to do so is actor and director Henry Kendall, who selects *Who's Who in the Theatre*.

2018: Novelist Chimamanda Ngozi Adichie receives the PEN Pinter Prize from Lady Antonia Fraser, Harold Pinter's widow, at an event at the British Library. In her acceptance speech, called 'Shut Up and Write', she talks about identity, the need to speak out politically and what it means to be an African feminist writer.

10

1896: The *New York Times* publishes its first 'Books' section, initially called the *Saturday Book Review Supplement* before morphing in later years into the *New York Times Book Review*. Contents include the feature 'Oscar Wilde's Forlorn State', focusing on the writer's incarceration in Reading Gaol, a humorous article about the importance of original thinking over using clichés ('Novelists' Stock Phrases'), ten unsigned book reviews, numerous short items of literary news, and a piece on the worrying threat to bookshops posed by growing numbers of department stores.

1939: George Orwell snaps the handle off his spade while working in the garden at his home in Wallington, Hertfordshire. During the day he prepares a trench for his broad beans, moves the henhouse (five eggs today) and notes the poor crop of onions and walnuts.

11

1931: George Bernard Shaw appears on the US radio station CBS, presenting his lecture in support of Stalin whom, like so many other left-leaning writers of the time (see 23 July), he has recently met in the USSR on a nine-day visit. 'Hello America!' he starts. 'Hello, all my friends in America! How are all you dear old boobs who have been telling one another for a month that I have gone dotty about Russia?' He praises communism, endorses Stalin and suggests skilled workmen looking for a job will certainly be able to find one in Russia. Shaw adds that 'the sun shines in Russia as on a country with which

God is well pleased'. CBS receives so many complaints about Shaw's talk that they swiftly invite Rev. Edmund A. Walsh, vice-president of Georgetown University, to put the other side of the story, during which he calls Shaw 'the licensed charlatan of English letters'.

12

1609: 'Three Blind Mice' appears for the first time in print in *Deuteromelia or The Seconde part of Musicks melodie*, edited by Thomas Ravenscroft. He may also have written both the lyrics and the tune. The original text runs:

Three Blinde Mice, Three Blinde Mice,
Dame Iulian, Dame Iulian,
The Miller and his merry olde Wife,
Shee scrapte her tripe licke thou the knife.

1654: A huge explosion in a convent in Delft in the Netherlands kills the up-and-coming Dutch painter Carel Fabritius aged thirty-two. Not much of his work survives, although he comes to the public eye again thanks to his work *The Goldfinch.* Painted a few months before his death, it shows the bird attached to a wall. The painting plays a key part in Donna Tartt's 2013 novel of the same name when – mild spoiler alert – it is stolen during a terrorist attack in the Metropolitan Museum in New York.

13

1913: J. M. Barrie's travelling 'village' cricket team the Allahakbarries play their last game. The author of *Peter Pan* is a decidedly average cricketer, but that does not stop him loving the sport. He puts together his equally decidedly average team, which is made up of a revolving roster of friends and fellow authors including Sir Arthur Conan Doyle (a decent batsman, who played for the MCC nearly 100 times and on 23 August 1900, took the wicket of the venerable W. G. Grace), P. G. Wodehouse, A. A. Milne, H. G. Wells and E. W. Hornung. Barrie's selection criteria are slightly unusual: he admits that he picks married men because he likes their wives, and single men whose appearance is a bit odd. The strange name of the team is derived from 'Allahu Akbar' (which

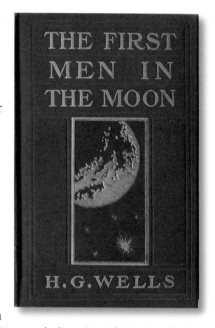

Barrie mistakenly believes means 'Heaven help us') with 'ries' tacked on at the end, thus coincidentally including the skipper's name.

1917: War poets Wilfred Owen, Siegfried Sassoon (a keen golfer) and Robert Graves meet up for the first and only time at Baberton Golf Club, Juniper Green, Edinburgh. It's not clear what they talk about, although Owen redrafts his poem 'Dulce et Decorum Est' two days later, but they obviously get on well as Graves invites Owen to his wedding the following 23 January 1918. A plaque at the golf club commemorating the meeting is erected exactly 100 years later in 2017.

14

1899: Anti-gravity metal Cavorite (when cool, anything it covers is no longer subject to the laws of gravity) is first produced. The discovery is made by accident by the fictional Dr Cavor in *The First Men in the Moon* (1901) by H. G. Wells, thus making a journey to the lunar surface feasible.

2019: Despite a rule change specifically banning joint winners, the Booker Prize for Fiction goes to joint winners Bernardine Evaristo for *Girl, Woman, Other*, and Margaret Atwood for *The Testaments*.

15

1764: Edward Gibbon is in Rome, specifically at the Franciscan Basilica of Santa Maria in Aracoeli. As he explains in his memoirs, inspiration strikes unexpectedly:

'It was at Rome, on the 15th of October, 1764, as I sat musing amidst the ruins of the Capitol, while the barefooted friars were singing vespers in the Temple of Jupiter, that the idea of writing the decline and fall of the city first started to my mind. But my original plan was circumscribed to the decay of the city rather than of the empire: and, though my reading and reflections began to point towards that object, some years elapsed, and several avocations intervened, before I was seriously engaged in the execution of that laborious work.'

(Though actually he's wrong, it was the Temple of Juno, not Jupiter.)

16

1959: Two days before his twentieth birthday, Lee Harvey Oswald starts a diary. On this day he records his arrival in Moscow from Helsinki and his preparations for his application to become a Soviet citizen.

17

1826: It's the wedding day for squabbling literary power couple Thomas Carlyle and Jane Welsh. The wedding night apparently does not go well, and the next morning a seemingly frustrated Carlyle destroys the flower garden at their Comely Bank home in Edinburgh.

1896: It's also not a good night for Anton Chekhov, whose new play *The Seagull* is booed by the audience at its St Petersburg premiere in the Alexandrinsky Theatre, probably because they misunderstand why the playwright has labelled it a 'comedy'. In a letter to a friend, he suggests the root of the problems: that he has played no part in casting, there is no new scenery and only two rehearsals, and the actors don't know their lines properly. After Act II, Chekhov leaves his seat

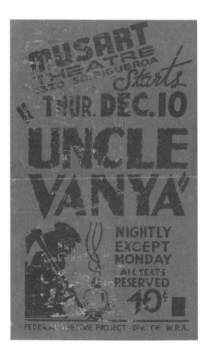

in the auditorium and makes himself scarce backstage, vowing never to write another play. Happily, he changes his mind to write *Uncle Vanya* and *The Cherry Orchard*.

18

1941: Canadian diplomat Charles Ritchie, long-time lover of the married novelist Elizabeth Bowen, is reading her book *The Death of the Heart* (1938). He realises that she has exactly replicated the furniture from her married home in the book, which is what Ritchie calls 'an unsparing portrait' of her husband Alan. He also recognises other elements that she has taken from real life, comparing the sensation of reading them to having eaten a complex meal whose ingredients have been previously seen in their raw form beforehand.

1806: War between a coalition of European countries and Napoleon's French forces is ongoing. The emperor's least disciplined troops – the so-called 'spoon guards' – break into Johann Wolfgang von Goethe's home in Weimar, which he shares with his mistress Christiane Vulpius. She barricades the kitchen and cellar and essentially drives them away. 'A frightful night,' he comments in his diary. The couple marry six days later.

19

1878: Henry James's friend Mrs Richard Greville visits George Eliot and her husband George Lewes and gifts them a copy of James's recent two-volume novel *The Europeans*. When she returns on 1 November, this time with James, Mr Lewes presses both books on James, unaware that he is their author. 'Take them away, please, away,' says Lewes. In his 1917 book *The Middle Years*, James takes up the story:

'Our hosts hadn't so much as connected book with author, or author with visitor, or visitor with anything but the convenience of his ridding them of an unconsidered trifle; grudging as they so justifiedly did the impingement of such matters on their consciousness. The vivid demonstration of one's failure to penetrate there had been in the sweep of Lewes's gesture, which could scarcely have been bettered by his actually wielding a broom.'

20

1793 (likely): Edward Rochester marries Bertha Mason in Charlotte Brontë's 1847 novel *Jane Eyre*, fifteen years before his wedding day with Jane in 1808.

1921: The Society of Bookmen, a club for people in the UK book trade including publishers, booksellers, literary agents, librarians and writers, meets for the first time. Among founding members present on this first occasion at novelist Hugh Walpole's home in London are John Galsworthy, Stanley Unwin and Harold Macmillan. The club is now known as the Book Society.

1928: In her review slot 'The Constant Reader' in the *New Yorker* magazine, Dorothy Parker gives *The House at Pooh Corner* by A. A. Milne an absolute mauling. At the point Pooh tells Piglet how he has adjusted his song 'The more it SNOWS' to make it more 'hummy', Parker says 'Tonstant Weader fwowed up'.

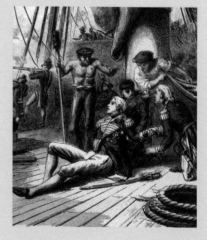

21

1805: Nelson's last journal entry, also known as 'Nelson's Prayer', is made on the morning of the Battle of Trafalgar:

'May the Great God whom I worship Grant to my Country and

for the benefit of Europe in General a great and Glorious Victory, and may no misconduct in any one tarnish it, and may humanity after Victory be the predominant feature in the British fleet, for myself individually I commit my Life to Him who made me, and may his blessing light upon my Endeavours for serving my Country faithfully. To Him I resign myself and the just cause which is Entrusted to me to Defend. Amen.'

With an eye on posterity, he has at least one additional copy made of it.

22

1885: French poet Arthur Rimbaud writes to his mother that he has decided to become a gun runner in Ethiopia.

23

1731: At around 2 a.m., a fire breaks out at Ashburnham House in Westminster, London. It is home to hundreds of priceless manuscripts, known as the Cotton Library after the great manuscript collector Sir Robert Cotton (1571–1631). Although some items are saved simply by being thrown out of windows, among those lost to the flames are *The Battle of Maldon* and Asser's *Life of Alfred*, which have only survived thanks to transcriptions. Among those saved is the vellum codex of *Beowulf*, now safely held at the British Library, although it is a bit singed around the edges.

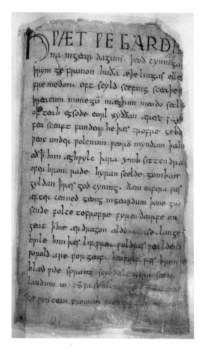

24

1958: Raymond Chandler starts writing his last novel, *Poodle Springs*. He only completes four chapters before he dies the following March. It is published in 1989, finished by Robert B. Parker.

25

1819: Percy Shelley composes his 'Ode to the West Wind' – 'If Winter comes, can Spring be far behind?' – apparently at a single sitting, in the Cascine Woods, near Florence.

1854: Some of the details of the calamitous Charge of the Light Brigade at the Battle of Balaclava on this day are cleared up in Victorian military hero Harry Flashman's recently discovered memoirs, recounted by George Macdonald Fraser in *Flashman at the Charge* (1973). Indeed, Flashy is reponsible for the charge itself. Having quaffed vast quantities of bad Russian champagne and consequently contracted dysentery, he develops a very bad case of wind, which alarms his horse and sets the historic events in train …

26

1900: Edith Wharton and Henry James begin their lasting literary friendship by correspondence. James writes to Wharton, twenty years his junior, about her new story *The Line of Least Resistance*:

Dear Mrs Wharton,

SCRIBNER'S

FOR MARCH NOW READY

Everybody is talking of "THE HOUSE OF MIRTH," by Edith Wharton in Scribner's Are you reading it?

I brave your interdiction & thank you both for your letter & for the brilliant little tale in the Philadelphia repository [Lippincott's]. The latter has an admirable sharpness & neatness, & infinite wit & point – it only suffers a little, I think, from one's not having a direct glimpse of the husband's provoking causes – literally provoking ones … The subject is really a big one for the canvas – that was really your difficulty. But the thing is done. And I applaud, I mean I value, I egg you on in, your study of the American life that surrounds you. Let yourself go in it & at it – it's an untouched field, really: the folk who try, over there, don't come within miles of any civilized, however superficially, any 'evolved' life. And use to the full your ironic and satiric gifts; they form a most valuable (I hold) & beneficent engine. Only, the Lippincott tale is a little hard, a little purely derisive. But that's because you're so young, &, with it, so clever. Youth is hard – & your needle-point, later on, will muffle itself in a little blur of silk. It is a needle-point! Do send me what you write, when you can kindly find time, & do, some day, better still, come to see yours, dear Mrs Wharton, most truly,

Henry James

They meet in person for the first time in December 1903.

27

1999: Marilyn Monroe's personal library comes to auction at Christie's. She was a keen reader, and the sale features a wide range of titles including *A Farewell to Arms* by Ernest Hemingway, Fannie Farmer's *The Boston Cooking-School Cook Book*, various books by Colette and a copy of James Joyce's *Ulysses*. The photo of Marilyn reading the Joyce which was taken by Eve Arnold for *Esquire* magazine in 1955 and has a pre-auction estimate of $300–500 actually goes for $9,200.

28

1853: Henry David Thoreau brings home around 700 copies of his book *A Week on the Concord and Merrimack Rivers* from his publisher; it is something of a dry run for his best-known work, *Walden*. He has paid for the printing of 1,000 copies, but it has not sold well. 'I now have a library of nearly nine hundred volumes,' he writes a little mournfully in his journal, 'over seven hundred of which I wrote myself.' But then he bucks himself up by adding more positively: 'Is it not well that the author should behold the fruits of his labor? Indeed, I believe that this result is more inspiring and better for me than if a thousand had bought my wares. It affects my privacy less and leaves me freer.'

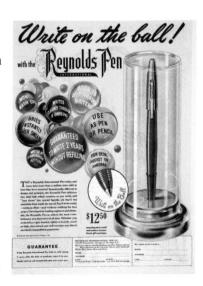

29

1945: It's not the first ballpoint pen to go on sale, but it is the first commercially successful one offering writers a genuine alternative to the fountain pen. It comes from Reynolds International

Pen Company, is designed by László Bíró, and is an immediate success from the moment it appears on this day in Gimbels department store, New York.

30

1811: Anonymously, Jane Austen self-publishes *Sense and Sensibility* in three volumes. 'I am never too busy to think of S&S. I can no more forget it, than a mother can forget her sucking child,' she writes to her sister, Cassandra.

1947: Bertolt Brecht makes an impish appearance before the House Un-American Activities Committee, choosing his words very carefully to outwit his questioners. So when he is asked if he is the author of a song which chief investigator Robert Stripling reads out in English translation ('Forward We've Not Forgotten') he says 'No, I wrote a German poem, but that is very different from this thing.' And when asked whether he has written anything revolutionary, Brecht replies: 'I have written a number of poems and songs and plays in the fight against Hitler, and of course they can be considered therefore as revolutionary, because I of course was for the overthrow of that government.' The following day Brecht flies to Europe and never returns to America.

31

1997: The third episode of season five of *Frasier* airs tonight. Niles is hosting a fundraising costume party for the Library Association. Invitees come as literary characters: Geoffrey Chaucer and the Wife of Bath (Frasier and Daphne), Cyrano de Bergerac (Niles), Sherlock Holmes (Martin, Frasier's dad), O from *Story of O* (Roz, Frasier's work colleague), and Waldo from the *Where's Waldo/Wally?* books (Bulldog, Frasier's fellow broadcaster).

FINAL WORDS

'Lord! Open the King of England's eyes'
William Tyndale (*c.* 6 October 1536)

'Ah, a German and a genius! A prodigy. Admit him'
Jonathan Swift (19 October 1745), learning that
George Frederic Handel had come to visit him

'Lord help my poor soul'
or, slightly less probably,
*'The arched heavens encompass me, and God has his
decree legibly written upon the frontlets of every created
human being, and demons incarnate, their goal will be
the seething waves of blank despair*
Edgar Allan Poe (7 October 1849)

'I have opened it'
Alfred Lord Tennyson (6 October 1892), perhaps referring
to the copy of *Cymbeline* that he had been trying to read
on his deathbed and with which he was buried

'What a life'
Radclyffe Hall (7 October 1943)

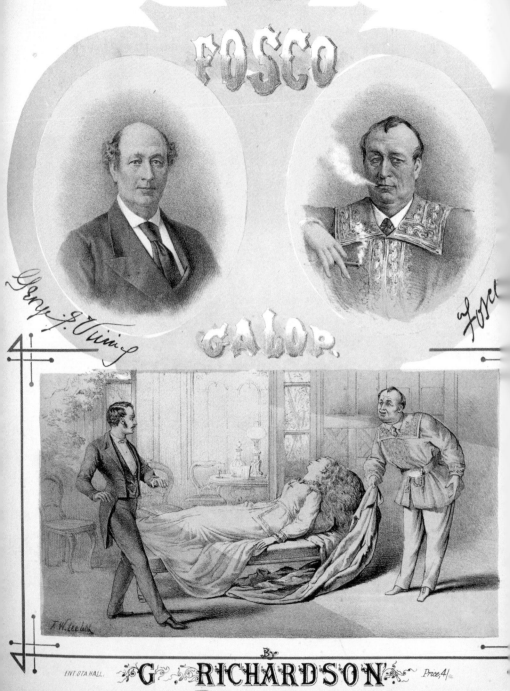

NOVEMBER

No shade, no shine, no butterflies, no bees,
No fruits, no flowers, no leaves, no birds! –
November!
'November' (1844) by Thomas Hood

Births
Margaret Mitchell (8 November 1900)
Astrid Lindgren (14 November 1907)
Roger Lancelyn Green (2 November 1918)
Margaret Atwood (18 November 1942)
Sharon Olds (19 November 1942)

Deaths
Washington Irving (28 November 1859)
Stieg Larsson (9 November 2004)
P. D. James (27 November 2014)
William Trevor (20 November 2016)
Jan Morris (20 November 2020)

First published/performed
26 November 1859: *The Woman in White* by Wilkie Collins
24 November 1877: *Black Beauty* by Anna Sewell
14 November 1883: *Treasure Island* by Robert Louis Stevenson
1 November 1895: *Jude the Obscure* by Thomas Hardy
22 November 1957: *Doctor Zhivago* by Boris Pasternak

1

1797: Jane Austen's supportive father, George, writes to publisher Thomas Cadell in London asking him if he might be interested in *First Impressions*, the manuscript that will later become *Pride and Prejudice*. 'I have in my possession a Manuscript Novel, comprised in three Vols about the length of Miss Burney's *Evelina*. As I am well aware of what consequence it is that a work of this sort should make it's first appearance under a respectable name I apply to you.' The offer is declined by return of post. It will be fourteen years before Jane publishes her first book, *Sense and Sensibility*.

2

1883: Poet Emma Lazarus reads her sonnet 'The New Colossus' at a fundraiser for the construction of the Statue of Liberty's pedestal. Largely neglected over the following decade, it then becomes a permanent part of the statue in 1903 when a plaque with the text is attached to its inner wall:

Not like the brazen giant of Greek fame,
With conquering limbs astride from land to land;
Here at our sea-washed, sunset gates shall stand
A mighty woman with a torch, whose flame
Is the imprisoned lightning, and her name
Mother of Exiles. From her beacon-hand
Glows world-wide welcome; her mild eyes command
The air-bridged harbor that twin cities frame.

'Keep, ancient lands, your storied pomp!' cries she
With silent lips. 'Give me your tired, your poor,
Your huddled masses yearning to breathe free,
The wretched refuse of your teeming shore.
Send these, the homeless, tempest-tost to me,
I lift my lamp beside the golden door!'

3

1871: Walt Whitman very gently turns down a marriage proposal from British superfan Anne Gilchrist, sometime next-door neighbour in Chelsea to Thomas and Jane Carlyle (see 17 October):

'I must at least show without further delay that I am not insensible to your love. I too send you my love. And do you feel no disappointment because I now write so briefly. My book is my best letter, my response, my truest explanation of all. In it I have put my body and spirit. You understand this better and fuller and clearer than any one else. And I too fully and clearly understand the loving letter it has evoked.

Enough that there surely exists so beautiful and a delicate relation, accepted by both of us with joy.'

It's not enough to put his admirer off, and her letters continue until she travels to America in 1876, when they meet and become just good friends.

1966: Georgette Heyer has lunch with Queen Elizabeth II at Buckingham Palace. It turns out she is the only woman among twelve other invitees. After the corgis bounce in, she sits next to Prince Philip at the meal but has very little conversation with the queen, writing to a friend in South Africa that: 'She kept on stealing sidelong looks at me, & blushing pink whenever I happened to catch her eye.' At Harrods' book department a few days later, the manager tells her that the queen has very recently been in to buy a dozen copies of Heyer's Regency romance *Frederica*.

4

Alice's adventures *Through the Looking-Glass* (1871) begin on this day. Lewis Carroll does not specify the date in the text, but in the first chapter it is implied that the next day is Guy Fawkes Day (boys outside are building bonfires in preparation). And in Chapter 6 Alice says she is seven years and

six months old – Alice Liddell, inspiration for the stories, was born on 4 May, again indicating 4 November, her half-birthday.

1930: Coincidentally, a young Alan Turing takes *Through the Looking Glass* out of the library at Sherborne School, where he is a pupil. The future ground-breaking computer scientist also takes out Carroll's less famous *The Game of Logic* (1886).

5

1699: Lemuel Gulliver arrives in Lilliput after a storm wrecks his ship in *Gulliver's Travels* (1726) by Jonathan Swift.

1718: Tristram Shandy is born, or as he puts it himself in *The Life and Opinions of Tristram Shandy, Gentleman* (1759–67) by Laurence Sterne: 'On the fifth day of November, 1718 … was I Tristram Shandy, Gentleman, brought forth into this scurvy and disastrous world of ours.'

1867: Harpooner Ned Land first sees the *Nautilus* in *Twenty Thousand Leagues under the Sea* (1870) by Jules Verne

1966: Book artist Tom Phillips begins the odyssey of his cult classic and what he called his 'strange labour', *A Humument: A Treated Victorian Novel*. At noon, he enters Austin's Furniture Repository on Peckham Rye and buys the second-hand book *A Human Document* (1892) by W. H. Mallock for threepence. Over the next fifty years,

he alters every page by painting, collage and cut-up techniques to produce a completely new volume, which is first published in 1973 and republished for the sixth and final time in 2016 in a completely transformed edition.

6

Count Dracula dies at the hands of Jonathan Harker and Quincey Morris in *Dracula* (1897) by Bram Stoker.

7

1924: F. Scott Fitzgerald writes to his editor Max Perkins to confirm he is definitely going to call his new novel *Trimalchio in West Egg*, and not *The Great Gatsby* (see 19 March).

2021: Novelist Joanne Harris chooses her writing shed as her castaway luxury on *Desert Island Discs*.

8

1602: Although its roots date back to the fourteenth century, the Bodleian Library in Oxford officially opens to scholars on this day thanks to the largesse of diplomat and lecturer Sir Thomas Bodley.

9

1947: Harold Nicolson – diplomat, writer, and husband of Vita Sackville-West – writes in his own diary about Samuel Pepys that he was 'a mean little man' and 'salacious in a grubby way' but grudgingly admits that at least he did keep working during the Great Plague.

10

1862: Dorian Gray's birthday in Oscar Wilde's novel, *The Picture of Dorian Gray* (1891).

1951: Managing director of Guinness Breweries Sir Hugh Beaver is on a shooting party in County Wexford, Ireland. After he misses several shots at a golden plover, a good-natured argument develops over which is Europe's fastest game bird. Later that evening he finds it impossible to track down the answer in any reference books and comes up with the idea of producing a book containing all such answers. He teams up with twins Norris and Ross McWhirter, owners of a fact-checking agency for newspapers and magazines, who compile *The Guinness Book of Records*, which is first published in August 1954. Without clarification of the fastest flying game bird.

1960: On its first day of publication and retailing at 3*s* 6*d*, *Lady Chatterley's Lover* sells 200,000 copies, mostly to men. Foyles in London sells its 300 copies in a quarter of an hour. The book has previously been banned since it was written in 1928; in Parliament the Lord Advocate is pressed on whether booksellers who sell copies of it will be punished, but says only that he is considering the matter.

2015: The Bodleian Library announces it has acquired its twelve millionth book, a copy of Shelley's 'Poetical Essay on the Existing

State of Things' – a small, twenty-page pamphlet featuring a ten-page poem – published in 1811 and long thought lost.

11

1920/1921: James Bond is born, though there's some discrepancy among Bond scholars as to precisely which year since his creator Ian Fleming never mentions it. In the 2006 film of *Casino Royale*, a shot of Bond's passport shows his birthday as 13 April 1968, a mash-up of the day the novel on which it is based was published in 1953, and Daniel Craig's birth year.

12

1943: *The Box of Delights* by John Masefield is dramatised for the first time. The series of six forty-minute radio broadcasts on *Children's Hour* on the BBC Home Service takes place weekly over November and December with Norman Shelley as the narrator, John Gilpin as Kay Harker, Robert Farquharson as Abner Brown and Hay Petrie as Cole Hawlings, with Charles Hawtrey as the Mouse.

13

1797: Around 4.30 p.m., Samuel Taylor Coleridge begins an extensive walk through the Quantock Hills in Somerset with William and Dorothy Wordsworth. During their excursion Coleridge comes up with the idea for his poem 'The Rime of the Ancient Mariner' after a discussion about a book William is reading by George Shelvocke, *A Voyage Round the World by Way of the Great South Sea* (1726). This features a sailor, Simon Hatley, earlier in the century who shoots a black albatross from the ship *Speedwell* near Cape Horn. The plan is to write it together and sell it to a magazine to offset the costs of the walking tour. This is how Wordsworth remembers its origins:

'Much the greatest part of the story was Mr Coleridge's invention; but certain parts I myself suggested: – for example, some crime was to be committed which should bring upon the old Navigator, as Coleridge afterwards delighted to call him, the spectral persecution, as a consequence of that crime, and his own wanderings. I had been reading in Shelvock's [sic] Voyages a day or two before that while doubling Cape Horn they frequently saw Albatrosses in that latitude, the largest sort of sea-fowl, some extending their wings twelve or fifteen feet. "Suppose", said I, "you represent him as having killed one of these birds on entering the South Sea, and that the tutelary Spirits of those regions take upon them to avenge the crime." The incident was thought fit for the purpose and adopted accordingly.'

14

1915: Around 1,200 copies of D. H. Lawrence's latest novel, *The Rainbow*, published on 30 September, are seized by police. They are then burnt by a hangman outside the Royal Exchange in London after Lawrence and his publisher Methuen are successfully prosecuted for its candid sexual content, not to mention the anti-war sentiments by the central lesbian character, Ursula. Herbert Muskett, leading the prosecution, says: 'Although there might not be an obscene word to be found in the book, it was in fact a mass of obscenity of thought, idea and action, wrapped up in language which in some quarters might be considered artistic and intellectual.' The judge, Sir John Dickinson, calls

it 'utter filth'. The book remains banned in Britain for another eleven years and is a turning point for Lawrence, who vows to leave Britain after the war ends.

1922: D. H. Lawrence returns a copy of James Joyce's *Ulysses* which his American agent has sent to him as a gift. 'It wearied me,' he writes.

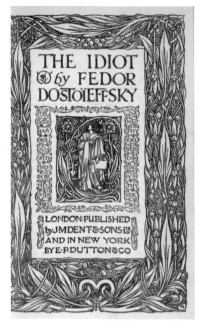

15

1762: The twenty-two-year-old James Boswell leaves his home city, Edinburgh, and travels to London. The journals he keeps over the next eight months, documenting society life in the capital in the eighteenth century, will make his name as a major diarist in his own right when they are discovered in the 1920s.

1856: Elizabeth Gaskell, in a letter to publisher George Smith: 'Oh! if once I have finished this biography [of Charlotte Brontë], catch me writing another! I shall be heaved overboard at last, like the ass belonging to the old man in the fable.'

1926: Ezra Pound, in a letter to James Joyce about his work in progress, later to become *Finnegans Wake*: 'I will have another go at it, but up to present I make nothing of it whatever. Nothing so far as I make out, nothing short of divine vision or a new cure for the clapp can possibly be worth all the circumambient peripherization.'

16

1849: Fyodor Dostoevsky is sentenced to death, charged with anti-government activities. As he is waiting to take his turn to be tied to the posts on 22 December, the firing squad is told to stand down – the tsar has theatrically already ordered their reprieve to be announced at the very last moment as a warning to others. The death sentence is commuted to four years' hard labour at a prison camp in Siberia followed by military service. He is released on 14 February 1854.

17

1603: Sir Walter Raleigh goes on trial for plotting treason against England's new monarch, James I. Found guilty, he is imprisoned in the Tower of London, where he writes his incomplete *Historie of the World*.

18

1926: 'I can forgive Alfred Nobel for inventing dynamite but only a fiend in human form could have invented the Nobel Prize,' says George Bernard Shaw, who rather reluctantly receives the said award for literature on this day. He turns down the prize money, saying that his readers provide him with all the income he needs, and requests that it goes towards paying for the translation of Swedish literature into English.

1948: Shirley Jackson writes to her parents that she has been to a local mothers' club meeting where nobody referred to her being a writer, 'as though it were not polite to talk about'.

2015: Ladybird books publishes its first series of books for adults, gentle parodies of the hugely successful series for children using the original artwork but with new text written by Joel Morris and Jason Hazeley. The eight books focus on Mindfulness, the Hipster, the Hangover, the Mid-Life Crisis, the Shed, the Wife, the Husband and Dating.

19

1833: Honoré de Balzac breaks the armchair in which he customarily writes. It is the second one to bite the dust during his career to date.

1919: On the Left Bank in Paris, Sylvia Beach opens Shakespeare and Company at 12 rue de l'Odéon; the shop soon becomes a magnet for many literary figures.

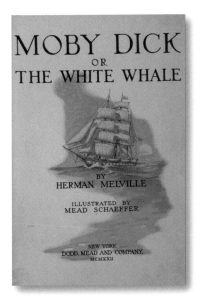

MOBY DICK
OR
THE WHITE WHALE

BY
HERMAN MELVILLE

ILLUSTRATED BY
MEAD SCHAEFFER

NEW YORK
DODD, MEAD AND COMPANY,
MCMXXII

1932: Eric Blair chooses his pen name 'George Orwell' from a selection he suggests in a letter to his agent, Leonard Moore. The others are Kenneth Miles, P. S. Burton and H. Lewis Allways. He tells his then girlfriend Eleanor Jacques that he likes it because it sounds 'like a good round English name'. It is probably partly a tribute to one of his favourite writers, George Gissing, and the result of a recent trip to Ipswich, through which runs the River Orwell.

2007: Amazon releases its first Kindle e-reader, retailing at $399, weighing ten ounces and selling out within six hours of hitting the shelves. 'This isn't a device,' enthuses Amazon CEO Jeff Bezos; 'it's a service.'

20

1820: American whaler the *Essex* is sunk in the southern Pacific Ocean after an attack by a sperm whale. It inspires Herman Melville to write *Moby-Dick* (1851).

1969: Asked by the *Toronto Star* for her predictions about literature in the 1970s, Joyce Carol Oates replies that she thinks they 'will be as exciting as the Sixties have been', with increasing numbers of small presses and magazines, and more experimental work published. She believes the novel is 'very much alive' and is hopeful that contemporary writers will be inspired by what she calls the 'leisurely and graceful storytelling' of the nineteenth century.

21

1879: Travel writer Isabella Bird complains to John Murray about a sexist review in *The Times* of her latest bestseller, *A Lady's Life in the Rocky Mountains*. The reviewer suggested that she has 'donned masculine habiliments for her greater convenience' while riding in Colorado. Bird tells Murray that it's an outrageous libel and encloses a note to be carried in the second edition which reads:

'For the benefit of other lady travellers, I wish to explain that my 'Hawaiian riding dress', a half-fitting jacket, a skirt reaching to the ankles, and full Turkish trousers gathered into a band with a frilling over the boots, is a thoroughly serviceable and feminine costume for mountaineering and other rough travelling, as in the Alps or any part of the world.'

1945: J. R. R. Tolkien and his wife Edith hold a coming-of-age party at their home for their son Christopher. At the bottom of the invitations, they add:

Carriages at midnight.
Ambulances at 2 a.m.
Wheelbarrows at 5 a.m.
Hearses at daybreak.

22

1962: As demanded by George Bernard Shaw in his 1950 will, a new edition of his play *Androcles and the Lion* is published which includes both traditional English spellings and one using a new phonetic alphabet called Shavian. Designed by Ronald Kingsley Read, it looks similar to the Pitman shorthand that Shaw used to write some of his works and diary entries.

1963: The sixty-nine-year-old Aldous Huxley, who has written about euthanasia in his novel *Brave New World* (1932) and his psychedelic experiences in *The Doors of Perception* (1953), is on his deathbed. As he approaches his final moments, he asks his wife Laura to give him LSD to ease his end. After two doses, he dies at 5.20 p.m. His death and that of fellow writer C. S. Lewis are eclipsed by the assassination of US President John F. Kennedy on the same day.

23

1621: Poet John Donne is elected Dean of St Paul's Cathedral in London. He holds this position until his death in 1631.

1852: Britain's first public pillar boxes appear (in St Helier, Jersey, and green rather than red) on the initiative of novelist Anthony Trollope, at this point in his life a high-ranking official in the General Post Office.

24

1997: The British Library opens its new St Pancras building in London, designed by Colin St John Wilson. More than 2,000 books – and a complimentary glass of champagne – are provided to the readers

within two hours of opening, the first item to be ordered being volume 1 of *Fifteenth Century Studies* (1978).

25

1862: Harriet Beecher Stowe, author of *Uncle Tom's Cabin*, travels to Washington, DC and meets President Abraham Lincoln. Her daughter Hattie, accompanying her, writes to her sister: 'It was a very droll time that we had at the White House I assure you ... I will only say now that it was all very funny and we were ready to explode with laughter all the while ... but we succeeded getting through it without disgracing ourselves.' It's not clear what is so funny, nor whether the much-reported story that when they first met Lincoln said 'So you are the little woman who wrote the book that started this great war' is in fact true.

1864: Popular actor John Wilkes Booth stars as Mark Antony in a production of Shakespeare's *Julius Caesar* at the Winter Garden Theatre in New York. It's a charity fundraiser to help erect a statue of Shakespeare in Central Park. John's brothers Junius and Edwin play Caesar and Brutus, a part that John apparently has always enjoyed performing. Five months later, John assassinates President Abraham Lincoln.

It's the Feast Day of St Catherine of Alexandria, patron saint of, among others, scribes, scholars, students, librarians, archivists, Balliol College Oxford, philosophers, stenographers, manuscripts and unmarried women.

26

1530: According to the Privy Purse expense accounts for Henry VIII, a certain Joly Jak receives five

shillings 'for bringing the king's
books from York Place to
Hampton Court'.

27

1895: Alfred Nobel makes his will,
unexpectedly leaving most of his
fortune for the foundation of a
series of prizes, including 'one part
to the person who, in the field
of literature, produced the most
outstanding work in an idealistic
direction'.

28

1955: Asked by executives at Ford to help come up with names for
their new car, American poet Marianne Moore suggests dozens of
possibilities in a series of letters over the autumn, including on this
day 'Mongoose Civique', 'Pastelogram' and 'Thunder Crester'. Ford
puts together a longlist of 6,000 options and unwisely opts for 'Edsel'.

28

1785: Incarcerated in the Bastille prison in Paris, the Marquis de
Sade puts the final touches to his *120 Days of Sodom or the School
of Libertinage*. The manuscript is not published until 1904.

1966: There's a strong literary flavour to the guest list of the great
and the good at Truman Capote's Black and White Ball at the Plaza
Hotel, New York. The social event of the year is held by the author to
celebrate the success of his previous year's book *In Cold Blood*, and
among the invitees are Norman Mailer, Edward Albee, James Baldwin,
Tennessee Williams, Harper Lee, Sir Isaiah Berlin, Noël Coward,
Christopher Isherwood, Alfred Knopf, James Michener, Arthur Miller,
George Plimpton, Philip Roth, John Steinbeck and William Styron.

29

1990: Roald Dahl is buried at his local church, St Peter and St Paul's, Great Missenden, Buckinghamshire, six days after his death in Oxford. His granddaughter describes the occasion as 'a sort of Viking funeral' since he is buried with a few of his favourite things, including snooker cues, a power saw, chocolate, HB pencils and some good-quality Burgundy wine.

30

It's Jonathan Swift's birthday, which he marks every year by reading aloud from the Book of Job, especially chapter 3, which contains the verse 'Let the day perish wherein I was born, and the night in which it was said, "There is a man child conceived."'

FINAL WORDS

*'I've had eighteen straight whiskies.
I think that's the record'*
Dylan Thomas (9 November 1953), attributed,
and even more dubious mathematically

*'You know, I'm not frightened. It's just that
I will miss you all so much!'*
Roald Dahl (23 November 1990), though after
a morphine injection he adds 'Ow, fuck'

*'We all reveal our manifestations.
This manifestation is over. That's all'*
or
'But the peasants, how do peasants die?'
Leo Tolstoy (20 November 1910)

*'I knew it. Born in a hotel room and, goddamn it,
dying in a hotel room'*
Eugene O'Neill (27 November 1953)

'Put that bloody cigarette out'
'Saki', aka Hector Munro (14 November 1916), shot by
a sniper during the Battle of Ancre, France

Mr. Fezziwig's Ball.

DECEMBER

In cold December fragrant chaplets blow,
And heavy harvests nod beneath the snow.
The Dunciad (1728) by Alexander Pope

Births
Anthony Powell (21 December 1905)
Rumer Godden (10 December 1907)
Naguib Mahfouz (11 December 1911)
Penelope Fitzgerald (17 December 1916)
Clarice Lispector (10 December 1920)

Deaths
Christina Rossetti (29 December 1894)
W. G. Sebald (14 December 2001)
Harold Pinter (24 December 2008)
Elisabeth Beresford (24 December 2010)
John Le Carré (12 December 2020)

First published/performed
20 December 1819: *Ivanhoe* by Sir Walter Scott
19 December 1843: *A Christmas Carol* by Charles Dickens
10 December 1884: *Adventures of Huckleberry Finn* by Mark Twain
28 December 1897: *Cyrano de Bergerac* by Edmond Rostand
9 December 1928: *Journey's End* by R. C. Sherriff

1

1971: The free online library Project Gutenberg (mission statement: 'To encourage the creation and distribution of eBooks') is founded by Michael Hart (1947–2011), thus effectively inventing the modern ebook. The American Declaration of Independence is its first text. Today it continues to be run entirely by volunteers.

1977: At Henry Williamson's memorial service at St Martin-in-the-Fields, London, the poet laureate Ted Hughes recounts how he remembers reading *Tarka the Otter* aged eleven, 'and for the next year read little else'. He describes it as 'something of a holy book, a soul-book, written with the life blood of an unusual poet'.

2

1802: Twenty-six-year-old Jane Austen accepts a proposal of marriage from twenty-one-year-old Harris Bigg-Wither, the younger brother of her friends Alethea and Catherine. She changes her mind overnight and retracts her decision the next morning. No details emerge about Austen's thoughts on either of her choices, although her niece Caroline goes on to write: 'Mr Wither was very plain in person – awkward, and even uncouth in manner – nothing but his size to recommend him.'

3

1926: At their home in Sunningdale, Berkshire, Agatha Christie's husband Archie asks her for a divorce. They quarrel. She disappears, and her abandoned car is found by a chalk quarry the following day ...

4

1849: Charlotte Brontë meets William Makepeace Thackeray for the first time at a dinner gathering. She records in a letter to her father that:

'He is a very tall man, above six feet high, with a peculiar face – not handsome – very ugly indeed – generally somewhat satirical and stern in expression, but capable also of a kind look ... It is better I should think to have him for a friend than an enemy, for he is a most formidable looking personage. I listened to him as he conversed with the other gentlemen – all he says is most simple but often cynical, harsh and contradictory.'

Lewis Melville's account in his 1899 *Life of William Makepeace Thackeray* reveals that:

'At dinner, Miss Bronte was placed opposite him. "And", said Thackeray, "I had the miserable humiliation of seeing her ideal of me disappearing, as everything went into my mouth, and nothing came out of it, until, at last, as I took my fifth potato, she leaned across, with clasped hands and tearful eyes, and breathed imploringly, Oh, Mr. Thackeray! Don't!"'

5

1945: Earlier in the autumn, novelist Aldous Huxley was hired by Walt Disney to work on a screenplay for a possible version of *Alice's Adventures in Wonderland* (working title: *Alice and the Mysterious Mr Carroll*), to be a mixture of animation and live action. Huxley delivers the first draft today, but Disney is not keen and they part company. None of Huxley's ideas survive into the animated feature when it is released in 1951.

6

1875: The SS *Deutschland* steamship runs aground in a snow blizzard on the Kentish Knock shoal. Of a total of 213 crew and passengers, only 135 survive. It inspires Gerard Manley Hopkins to compose one

of his most famous poems, 'The Wreck of the Deutschland', written the following year but not published until 1918. The poem also features in *The Girls of Slender Means* by Muriel Spark, in which it is recited by elocution teacher Joanna.

7

1845: Henry Wadsworth Longfellow is in a quandary. 'I know not what name to give it,' he confides to his journal, 'not my new baby, but my new poem. Shall it be "Gabrielle", or "Celestine", or "Evangeline"?' It is contestant number three, 'Evangeline, a Tale of Acadie', which is published two years later with the memorable opening line 'This is the forest primeval.'

8

1660: The first known woman appears professionally on a public stage in an English play. Unfortunately, it's not clear exactly who plays Desdemona in the production of Shakespeare's *Othello* at Thomas Killigrew's Vere Street Theatre – it is either Anne Marshall or Margaret Hughes.

1915: 'In Flanders Fields' by Canadian writer and surgeon John McCrae first appears, anonymously, in *Punch* magazine. McCrae writes the famous words after noticing how quickly poppies are springing up near new graves while officiating at the 3 May burial of his friend and brother-in-arms Alexis Helmer at the Second Battle of Ypres. McCrae dies on 28 January 1918, and is buried with full military honours.

1956: T. S. Eliot meets Igor Stravinsky for tea at the Savoy Hotel, London. After a slow start – Eliot has been expecting somebody taller; Stravinsky finds him intellectually intimidating – they bond over a shared love of the music of Richard Wagner and dance. Two years later to the day, they meet up for dinner again, and Eliot admits he cannot recite his poems off by heart since he keeps rewriting them.

9

1854: Alfred, Lord Tennyson's poem 'The Charge of the Light Brigade' is published in *The Examiner*, a week after he writes it. His inspiration is an article in *The Times* about the famous episode at Balaclava in the Crimean War two months earlier (see 25 October).

10

2013: Many years after Nelson Mandela first recites it to fellow inmates during their incarceration on Robben Island, US President Barack Obama recites the final stanza of 'Invictus' (1888) by William Henley at the statesman's South African memorial service. Prince Harry also uses phrases from it for chapter headings in his 2023 memoir *Spare*.

11

1992: Journalist Terence Blacker comes up with the term 'Aga saga' in a column for *Publishing News*, applying it in particular to the middle-class world of the novels by Joanna Trollope.

12

1969: In response to a letter from the Academy of American Poets asking him which books he would urge his students to read if he were an English teacher in high school, poet Thom Gunn replies with the following list:

The Poet's Tongue edited by W. H. Auden and John Garrett
The Bob Dylan Song Book
The Beatles Song Book
Wilfred Owen's *Collected Poems*
D. H. Lawrence's *Collected Poems*
Selected Poems by Ezra Pound
The Back Country by Gary Snyder
Howl and Other Poems, and *Planet News* by Allen Ginsberg
Ariel by Sylvia Plath
Lupercal or *Selected Poems* by Ted Hughes

13

The last illustration of Pooh and Piglet walking into the sunset in the Hundred Acre Wood in A. A. Milne's *Winnie-the-Pooh* is sold by Bonhams at auction for US$220,000. The pen-and-ink sketch on board by Ernest Shepard is signed by the artist and includes additional notes in pencil.

14

1908: Edith Wharton writes her poem 'Survival'.

When you and I, like all things kind or cruel,
The garnered days and light evasive hours,
Are gone again to be a part of flowers
And tears and tides, in life's divine renewal,

If some grey eve to certain eyes should wear
A deeper radiance than mere light can give,
Some silent page abruptly flush and live,
May it not be that you and I are there?

1922: Virginia Woolf meets Vita Sackville-West at a dinner party hosted by Woolf's brother-in-law Clive Bell. First impression: 'She is a grenadier; hard; handsome; manly; inclined to double chin.'

1926: Ten days after going missing, Agatha Christie reappears in Harrogate at the Swan Hydropathic Hotel, nearly 200 miles away from her home. She has booked in as Mrs Teresa Neele (the same surname as her husband's mistress) and given her address as Cape Town, South Africa.

15

1924: F. Scott Fitzgerald sends a cable to his editor, Max Perkins, finally admitting defeat in the author's bid to not call his novel *The Great Gatsby* (see 19 March and 7 November).

2001: Alan Bennett makes a list in his diary of words only used at Christmas time, including tidings, abiding, swaddling, lo!, and abhors. Additionally, he notes that carols are full of titles for poor novels.

16

1901: Beatrix Potter's instinct to back her first book *The Tale of Peter Rabbit* and self-publish it is recognised by publisher Frederick Warne. He writes to her on this day offering a contract for a full-colour version of what he calls her 'Bunny book' with less text. 'Of course we cannot tell whether the work is likely to run to a second edition or not,' he warns, 'and therefore we fear it might not provide a reasonable remuneration for you.'

17

2007: George R. R. Martin tells his fans in a blog post that there is no news ('No good news. No bad news. No news of any sort') about a possible HBO adaption of his *A Song of Ice and Fire* saga. He says he honestly doesn't even know when there will be news.

18

1679: At about 8 p.m., the first poet laureate, John Dryden, is attacked in London. He is on his way back from Will's Coffee House to his home on Gerrard Street when three assailants mug and badly beat him up in the alley by the Lamb & Flag in Rose Street, Covent Garden. His offer of a £50 reward for information leading to the identification of his attackers (or a royal pardon if one of them owns up) goes unclaimed. Dryden has recently badmouthed Charles II, the Earl of Rochester and one of the king's mistresses, Louise de Kérouaille, the Duchess of Portsmouth, in a

pamphlet called 'An Essay upon Satyr'. Scholars suggest Rochester probably organised the assault as a punishment beating. A plaque at the pub commemorates the event but gives the wrong day (it says 19 December).

1946: Ace American fighter pilot Eddie Rickenbacker flies over Broadway and scatters the ashes of short story writer Damon Runyon, as directed by his son Damon Runyon, Jr.

19

1686: Robinson Crusoe (in the eponymous 1719 story by Daniel Defoe) leaves the island after twenty-eight years, two months and nineteen days.

1948: Susan Sontag puts together a TBR list of around 100 titles, including:

The Counterfeiters by André Gide
Tar by Sherwood Anderson
The Island Within by Ludwig Lewisohn
Sanctuary by William Faulkner
Esther Waters by George Moore

Diary of a Writer by Fyodor Dostoevsky
Against the Grain by Joris-Karl Huysmans
The Disciple by Paul Bourget
Poems by Dante, Ariosto, Tasso, Tibullus, Heine, Pushkin, Rimbaud, Verlaine, Apollinaire
Plays by Synge, O'Neill, Calderón, Shaw and Hellman

20

The Dark Is Rising by Susan Cooper begins, on the eve of the winter solstice which is also the snowy eleventh birthday of the main protagonist Will Stanton. The 2022 twelve-part BBC radio adaption also starts on this day on the World Service.

21

1872: After some confusion over dates, Phileas Fogg returns to the Reform Club in London having been *Around the World in Eighty Days*. Jules Verne's travel tale is first serialised in the Paris newspaper *Le Temps*, timed to coincide with the return of Fogg after his adventures.

22

1827: As brisk as bees, if not altogether as light as fairies, the members of the Pickwick Club travelling society assemble and head to Muggleton in the festive Christmas chapter of *The Pickwick Papers* (1836) by Charles Dickens.

LE TOUR DU MONDE EN QUATRE-VINGTS JOURS

23

2001: Appearing on BBC Radio 4's Desert Island Discs, Jamie Oliver tells host Sue Lawley that he's not going to choose a book to take with him as he doesn't read books, but if pressed would take a picture book. He explains that he's slightly dyslexic and reading makes him fall asleep. Other reluctant book-takers over the years include showjumper Harvey Smith (who simply declines to take one), writers Tariq Ali and David Walliams (who turn down the offer of the Bible) and George Clooney (who asks for *War and Peace* largely on the basis of requiring additional amounts of toilet paper).

24

1956: Writer Michael Bond is looking for Christmas stocking-filler presents for his wife in Selfridges on London's Oxford Street. He spots the last teddy bear on a shelf and, feeling sorry for it, buys it on impulse. He calls him Paddington after his local railway station ...

1881: Oscar Wilde leaves England aboard the SS *Arizona* and heads to America for a long lecture tour, arriving on 2 January, when he supposedly tells a customs officer: 'I have nothing to declare but my genius.' Ship's captain George Siddons Murray is among the passengers and crew who do not enjoy having Oscar on board, apparently commenting: 'I wish I had that man lashed to the bowsprit on the windward side.'

25

1878: Louisa May Alcott replies to a Miss Churchill who has written to her asking for advice about becoming a writer. 'There is no *easy* road to successful authorship; it has to be earned by long & patient labor, many disappointments, uncertainties & trials. Success is often a lucky accident, coming to those who may not deserve it, while others who do have to wait & hope till they have earned it. This is the best sort & the most enduring.' With commendable honesty, she adds: 'Though I do not enjoy writing "moral tales" for the young, I do it because it pays well.'

26

1666: Playwright Aphra Behn is working as a spy (codename 'Astrea') in the Netherlands for Charles II's government, which is keen to discover the strength of possible conspiracies there to remove the king from the throne. However, by this date she has run out of money and writes to Henry Bennet, Lord Arlington from Antwerp, asking for some to be sent urgently:

'Pardon me Sir that I aply myself to your Lordship: as the ffountaine from whence all the marcy I can expect (it seemes) must spring ... tis true I am sent for home: but tis as true that they knew well I had not money enough to com withall: I could not Beg nor starve heare ... if your Lordship will be pleasd to lett me have a Bill upon mr shaw for on[e] 100 pound more, of which my friend shall have part ... for god of heavens sake Sir take Pity on me; let me be usd like a Christian & one who would venture her life to gaine your ffavorable opinion & to be permitted amongst the number of my Lord your Lordships most ffaithfull & humble servant: A. Behne ... I humbly beg your Lordship to be speedy least I eate out my head.'

1959: A busy Boxing Day for Sylvia Plath, who makes fish soup, meatloaf, oatmeal cookies, apple cakes and bread stuffing.

27

1904: It's opening night at the Abbey Theatre in Dublin. One of the co-founders is poet and playwright W. B. Yeats. Of the three plays on this first bill two are by Yeats (*On Baile's Strand* and *Cathleen ni Houlihan*) and the third is *Spreading the News* by theatre impresario and writer Isabella Augusta, Lady Gregory, another co-founder of the Abbey.

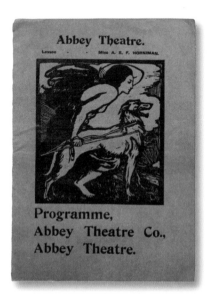

Programme, Abbey Theatre Co., Abbey Theatre.

28

1817: Painter Benjamin Haydon invites some of his poet friends – including essayist Charles Lamb, William Wordsworth and John Keats – to dine at his new home in Lisson Grove, London. He is keen to show them his latest work in progress, the huge *Christ's Entry into Jerusalem*, not least because he has painted the poets into the scene. Haydon writes of the dinner's success later in his journal:

'The immortal dinner came off in my painting-room, with Jerusalem towering up behind us as a background. Wordsworth was in fine cue, and we had a glorious set-to – on Homer, Shakespeare, Milton, and Virgil. Lamb got exceedingly merry and exquisitely witty; and his fun in the midst of Wordsworth's solemn intonations of oratory was like the sarcasm and wit of the fool in the intervals of Lear's passion … It was indeed an immortal evening. Wordsworth's fine intonation as he quoted Milton and Virgil, Keats' eager, inspired look, Lamb's faint sparkle of lambent humour, so speeded the stream of conversation, that in my life I never passed a more delightful time.'

29

1863: Around 7,000 people turn out for William Thackeray's funeral in Kensington Gardens, London, with 2,000 also attending his burial at Kensal Green Cemetery. His somewhat early death at the age of fifty-two is at least partly attributable to overeating and deliberately avoiding exercise.

30

1816: Mary Wollstonecraft Godwin marries Percy Shelley, two months after the suicide of his pregnant wife, Harriet.

1935: At 2.45 a.m., writer Antoine de Saint-Exupéry crash-lands his plane, the *Simoun*, in the Libyan desert. He and his navigator-engineer André Prévot have been flying for nearly twenty hours as they take part in the long-distance Paris-to-Saigon race. The crash leaves them with a pint of coffee in a flask, half a pint of white wine, some grapes and an orange, plus a small amount of medicine. They are rescued four days later by Bedouin tribesmen. Saint-Exupéry writes about the experience in his memoir *Wind, Sand and Stars* (1939) and recycles it for his novella *Le Petit Prince* or *The Little Prince (1943).*

31

1913: In his 'Locked Diary', E. M. Forster looks back on the previous year, especially the inspiration to write his novel *Maurice* after a liberating meeting on the day in question with gay activist Edward Carpenter:

'Maurice born on Sept. 13th. He tells the mood that created him. But will he ever be happy. He has become an independent existence … Forward rather than back. Edward Carpenter! Edward Carpenter! Edward Carpenter!'

1974/5: At the end of the 'End of the World' New Year's Party in Zadie Smith's *White Teeth*, Archie Jones meets Clara Bowden.

32

Hogswatchnight, the main winter and New Year festival in Terry Pratchett's *Discworld* novels, the night when the Hogfather delivers presents to children.

FINAL WORDS

'I am about to take my last voyage,
a great leap in the dark'
Thomas Hobbes (4 December 1679)

'Iam moriturus'
Dr Samuel Johnson (13 December 1784),
which translates as 'I who am about to die'

'How gratifying'
Robert Browning (12 December 1889) on receiving
positive reviews of his latest book, *Asolando*

'What's that? Does my face look strange?'
Robert Louis Stevenson (3 December 1894),
collapsing from a likely cerebral haemorrhage

'I love everybody. If ever I had an enemy, I should hope
to meet and welcome that enemy to heaven'
Christina Rossetti (29 December 1894)

PICTURE LIST

2. Customers inside a bookshop, from *The Story-Teller*, London: E. Nister, 1899. 12809.t.46.

3. Woman reading a book by Harry Clarke in *The Year's at the Spring*, London: G. G. Harrap & Co., 1920. 11603.h.21.

8. Illustration from *Frankenstein, or the Modern Prometheus*, 1831. 1153.a.9.(1).

10. George Eliot, *Middlemarch. A study of provincial life*, London: William Blackwood & Sons, 1871, 72. Cup.404.b.11.

11. Lord Byron, from *English poets. Twelve essays ... With twelve portraits*, London: Frederick Bruckmann, 1876. 1560/4193

12. A rear view of Raffles' house at Pematang Balam, West Sumatra, *c.* 1823. WD 2976.

13. Charles Darwin, from *The Origin of Species by Means of Natural Selection*, New York: H. M. Caldwell Co., 1898. 7006. ppp.42.

14. Illustration by W. H. Mote to accompany Robert Browning's poem 'My Lost Duchess', from *The Loves of the Poets; or, portraits of ideal beauty*, London, 1858. 11602.i.28.

16. *Tales of wonder!* from James Gillray, *The caricatures of Gillray; with historical and political illustrations, biographical anecdotes and notices*, London, 1818. 745.a.6 pl. 8.

17. Daniel Defoe, *The Life and Strange Surprising Adventures of Robinson Crusoe*, London: J. M. Dent & Co., 1905. Illustration by J. Ayton Symington. 012612.ee.9.

19. Entrance to Poets' Corner Westminster Abbey showing the busts of John Dryden, Ben Johnson, Abraham Cowley and others. Coloured aquatint by J. Bluck after A. Pugin, 1811. Wellcome Collection, London.

21. The Peacock Meal, 1914, (l–r) Victor Plarr, Thomas Sturge Moore, William Butler Yeats, Wilfrid Scawen Blunt, Ezra Pound, Richard Aldington, F.S. Flint. Private collection.

24. D. H. Lawrence, from *Britannia*, 18 January 1929. HIU.LON 810 (1929).

25. *Frost Fair*, 1684 pamphlet. Maps K.Top.27.39.

29. Illustration by Gwynedd M. Hudson from *Alice's Adventures in Wonderland*, London: Hodder and Stoughton, 1922. YA.1997.b.4119.

30. Mrs Isabella Beeton, *Beeton's Book of Household Management*, London: S. O. Beeton, 1859–61. C.133.c.5.

32. Shakespeare's House Stratford Upon Avon, c. 1770–1800. Maps K.Top.42.86.b.

33. *Midnight Race on the Mississippi*, 1875, lithograph, Metropolitan Museum of Art, New York. Bequest of Adele S. Colgate, 1962 (63.550.96).

34. Percy Bysshe Shelley, from *The Poetical Works of Percy Bysshe Shelley*, London: E. Moxon, 1839. 11611.df.18.

36. Miss Evans, from *Agatha*, London: Trübner & Co., 1869 (1889?). Ashley 712

37. Compton Mackenzie, *Whisky Galore*, London: Chatto & Windus, 1947. NN.37859.

38. William Shakespeare, *The Tragedie of King Richard the Second*, London, 1597. Huth 46.

39. Illustration by Albert Fourié, from *Madame Bovary*, Paris: A. Quantin, 1885. Tab.501.a.5.

40. D. H. Lawrence, *The White Peacock*, New York: Duffield & Co, 1911. Cup.403.e.12.

41. Autograph manuscript of Lewis Carroll's *Alice's Adventures Under Ground (in Wonderland)*, Oxford, 1862–64. Add. 46700, f.45v.

42. Thomas Hardy, *Far from the Madding Crowd*, London: Sampson Low, Marston, Searle & Rivington, 1889. RB.23.a.15316.

43. Charles Dickens, *Sketches by Boz*, 2nd edition, London: John Macrone, 1837. Illustration by George Cruikshank. 838.f.23.

44. Victor Hugo, *Les Misérables*, Paris: J. Hetzel et A. Lacroix, 1862. Illustration by Brion. Bibliothèque Nationale de France, Paris. Fonds Heure Joyeuse (2013-372294).

45. Oscar Wilde, New York, 1882. Add. 81785 (1b).

46. Ian Fleming, *Casino Royale*, London: Jonathan Cape, 1953. Cup.410.f.557.

47. Gutenberg Bible, Mainz, 1455. C.9.d.3.

48. Nikolai V. Alekseev, *Couple at Table*, 1930, woodcut for Nikolai Gogol, *Dead Souls*. Philadelphia Museum of Art. Gift of the American Russian Institute, 1941 (1941-104-1).
49. The Theatre Royal, Drury Lane, London, on fire, from *Authentic Account of the Fire...*, London: W. Glendinning, for T. Broom, 1809. 1430.a.22.
50. Sylvia Plath and Ted Hughes, Massachusetts, 20 May 1959. Bridgeman Images.
51. Illustration by John Tenniel, from *Through the Looking-Glass, and what Alice found there*, London: Macmillan & Co., 1897. 012808.eee.57.
52. H. G. Wells, *The Invisible Man. A grotesque romance*, London: C. A. Pearson, 1897. 012625.h.20.
54. P. G. Wodehouse, *Thank You, Jeeves*, London: Herbert Jenkins, 1934. Photo Rod Collins/Alamy Stock Photo.
57. Illustration, from *A Study in Scarlet*, in Warwick House Library, 1891. 012208.g.7/1.
60. W. M. Thackeray, *Vanity Fair*, London: Bradbury & Evans for Punch, 1847. Private collection.
61. Charles Dickens, from *The life of Charles Dickens*, London: Chapman & Hall, 1872–74. Dex.316 f.129.
62. Cartoon by Felix Mahony in *How to Run Libraries*, New York, 1901. Library of Congress, Prints and Photographs Division, Washington, D.C.
63. William Wordsworth, from *English poets. Twelve essays ...*, London: Frederick Bruckmann, 1876. 1560/4193.
64. Josephine Tey, *The Franchise affair*, London: Penguin Crime, 1951. Private collection.
65. F. Scott Fitzgerald, *The Great Gatsby*, London: Chatto & Windus, 1926. Private collection.
67. Illustration from *Twenty thousand Leagues under the Seas*, London: Sampson Low & Co, 1873. 12516.g.21.
68. Lady Caroline Lamb, from *Finden's Illustrations of the Life and Works of Lord Byron*, London: John Murray, 1833. 841.m.19.
69. Lawrence Ferlinghetti with copies of *Howl*, 1957. Photo Bob Campbell/San Francisco Chronicle via Getty Images.
71. 'Trial of Oscar Wilde', from *The Illustrated*

Police News, London, 4 May, 1895. Colindale 066157.
73. Arnold Bennett, *Buried Alive*, London: Amalgamated Press, 1910. 012604.e.1/78.
74. *Rubáiyát of Omar Khayyám*, Boston: Houghton, Mifflin & Co., 1884. C.188.c.27.
76. George Bernard Shaw in his garden hut, June 1937. Masheter Movie Archive/Alamy Stock Photo
77. Illustration by Weedon Grossmith from *The Diary of a Nobody*, Bristol: J. W. Arrowsmith, 1892. 012314.f.25.
78. George Orwell, *Nineteen Eighty-Four*, London: Secker & Warburg, 1949. Image courtesy Heritage Auctions, HA.com.
79. *Poems of Petrarch*, Italy, late 15th c. Add. 38125.
80. Samuel Johnson by Thomas Bewick, from *Bewick's Woodcuts*, London, 1870. 1784.b.13.
81. Illustration by Charles Robert Leslie, from *The Bride of Lammermoor*, Edinburgh: Adam & Charles Black, 1886. W80/9727.
83. Caen wood from Hampstead Heath near London, pub. 20 June, 1799. Maps K.Top.30.31.e.
85. Autograph manuscript of George Frederic Handel's, *The Messiah*, 1741. R.M.20.f.2, 132v.
86. *Daily Mirror* report on the loss of *Titanic*, London, 17 April 1912. E50002-51.
87. A View of Ulswater, in Cumberland, John Laporte, 1795. Maps K.Top.10.45.e.
88. Geoffrey Chaucer, from *The Canterbury Tales*, Westminster: William Caxton, c. 1476–77. 167.c.26.
89. Thomas Mann, *The Magic Mountain*, New York: Alfred A. Knopf, 1939. Private collection.
91. Thomas Stevens, from *Around the World on a Bicycle, from San Francisco to Teheran*, London: Sampson Low & Co, 1887. 10027.g.6.
92. Illustration, from 'The adventure of the final problem' in *The Strand*, London: George Newnes, 1893. P.P.6004.glk.
96. Lyman Frank Baum, *The Wizard of Oz*, Indianapolis: Bobbs-Merrill Co.; London: Hodder & Stoughton, 1906. Illustration by W. W. Denslow. 12813.tt.15.
98. *The Natural History of the Ordinary Cetacea or Whales*, The Naturalist's Library, 1843. 1150.a.4.
99. Muriel Spark, *The Comforters*, London: Macmillan, 1957. Private collection.

100. Bram Stoker, *Dracula*, London: William Rider & Son, 1919. X.907/9316.
101. Illustration by Edward Burne-Jones from *Franklin's Tale* in *The Works of Geoffrey Chaucer*, Hammersmith: Kelmscott Press, 1896. C.43.h.19.
103. 'The great actor, or Mr. Punch in all his glory' by Robert Cruikshank from *The English Spy*, London: Sherwood, Jones & Co., 1825–26. C.58.g.15.
104. 'Toad on a grassy bank' from *Album of Paintings by Kyomjae*, Korea, mid-18th c. Or. 5713, ff.9v–10.
105. *Diamond Sutra*, China, 868. Or. 8210/P.2.
106. Samuel Pepys, from *Memoirs of Samuel Pepys*, London: H. Colburn, 1825. 1321.h.22.
107. *Views of Chetham's Hospital & Library*, Manchester, early 20th c. LB.31.a.6849.
109. Mr. Davies' Shop, Russell Street, from *Old and New London: A Narrative of Its History, Its People, and Its Places. W and the Western Suburbs*, Vol. III. page 271, London: Cassell, Petter, & Galpin, 1873–78. 10348.f.12.
110. *Le Spectre de la Rose* by George Barbier, from *Designs on the Dances of Vaslav Nijinsky*, London, Paris, 1913. L.R.28.a.14.
112. (left) Elizabeth Barrett Browning, from *Portrait Gallery of Eminent Men and Women of Europe*, vol. II, New York, 1872–74. 10604.g.10. (right) Robert Browning, from *A New Spirit of the Age*, London, 1844. 1203.g.3.
113. James Hilton, *Lost Horizon*, London: Macmillan, 1933. Private collection.
114. New York Public Library, c. 1911. Library of Congress, Prints and Photographs Division, Washington, D.C.
115. Henry Williamson, *Tarka the Otter*, London: Puffin Story books, 1949. Jacket design by C. F. Tunnicliffe. Private collection.
116. View of Whitby Abbey, by Buckler; engraved by Reeve, 1812. Maps K.Top.44.53.f.
117. John Steinbeck, *Of Mice and Men*, New York: Covici-Friede, 1937. Image courtesy Heritage Auctions, HA.com.
118. Christopher Marlowe, *The Tragicall History of the Life and Death of Doctor Faustus*, 1620. C.39.c.26.
120. Charles Baudelaire, *Les Fleurs du mal*, vol. I. Paris: Ambroise Vollard, 1916.

Illustration by Emile Bernard. Paris Musées/ Petit Palais, musée des Beaux-Arts de la Ville de Paris.
122. 'The lying-in-state and funeral of the late Victor Hugo in Paris', from *The Graphic*, 1885. Maison de Victor Hugo, Hauteville House (2017.0.3656.1). Paris Musées/ Maisons de Victor Hugo Paris, Guernesey.
124. Frédéric-Auguste Cazals, *Paul Verlaine dans un paysage hivernal*, 1886–1896. Musée Carnavalet, Histoire de Paris (D.14779). Paris Musées/Musée Carnavalet, Histoire de Paris.
125. J. D. Salinger, *The Catcher in the Rye*, Boston: Little Brown, 1951. Jacket design by Michael Mitchell. Private collection.
126. *Lindisfarne Gospels*, England, 8th c. Cotton Nero D. IV, f.138v.
128. Anthony Trollope, *John Caldigate*, London: Routledge & Co., 1880. 12619.i.6.
129. *Paradise Lost* by Samuel Gribelin, after L. Chéron, from *The Poetical Works of Mr. John Milton*, London: Jacob Tonson, 1720. 83.k.19 book 7, 275.
130. James Joyce by Berenice Abbott, from the *Time Reading Program*, 1965. Library of Congress, Prints and Photographs Division, Washington, D.C.
131. William Mudford, *An Historical Account of the Campaign in the Netherlands*, in 1815, London: Henry Colburn, 1817. 193.e.9.
132. Samuel Johnson, *A Dictionary of English Language*, London: J. & P. Knapton, 1755–56. 680.k.12.
133. Mark Twain, *A Connecticut Yankee in King Arthur's Court*, New York: Charles L. Wevster & Co, 1889. Image courtesy Heritage Auctions, HA.com.
134. Anne Bradsheet, *Several Poems Compiled With Great Wit*, Boston, 1678. Library of Congress, Washington, D.C.
138. Illustration by Kate Greenaway, from *The Pied Piper of Hamelin*, London: Routledge, 1889. 11648.f.39.
140. Illustration by Alice B. Woodward, from *The Peter Pan Picture Book*, London: G. Bell & Sons, 1907. 12812.bb.20.
141. C. J. Visscher, A view of London showing the Globe Theatre, from *Londinum Florentissima Britannia Urbs*, 1616. Maps C.5.a.6.
142. Illustration from *Far From the Madding Crowd*, London: Sampson Low, Marston,

Searle & Rivington, 1889. RB.23.a.15316.
143. A bouquet of flowers, from *Album Vilmorin*, Paris, 1850. N.Tab.2004/11.
144. Illustration by Eric Kennington, from *Seven Pillars of Wisdom*, London: Jonathan Cape, 1935. C.116.c.7. Reproduced with permission of the Estate of Eric Kennington.
146. Reading Room at the British Museum, from *Free Public Libraries, their organisation, uses and management*, London: Simpkin, Marshall & Co., 1886. 11902.b.52.
147. Map of Pitcairn Island, from *An Account of the Voyages Undertaken by the Order of His Present Majesty*, London: W. Strahan and T. Cadell, 1773. Asia, Pacific & Africa W 7140.
148. *Anne Lister of Shibden Hall*, 1822, watercolour. Calderdale, West Yorkshire Archive Service.
149. *Mad Hatter's tea party* by Sir John Tenniel, from *The Nursery*, London: Macmillan & Co., 1890. Cup.410.g.74.
151. East Front of the new Theatre Royal, Covent Garden, London, 1809. Maps K.Top.25.19.1.c.
152. Pigs from *Dairy Farming, being the theory, practice and methods of dairying*, London: Cassell & Co, 1883–85. 7293.m.15.
153. Illustration from *Burns' Cottage: the story of the birthplace of Robert Burns, from ... June 1756 until the present day, etc.*, Glasgow: David Bryce and Son, 1904. 10855.aa.37.
155. Arthur Conan Doyle with physic extra, c. 1922, from *A Collection of Psychic Photographs, 1870–1930*. Cup.407.a.1.
156. Bayeux Tapestry, Duke William and his half-brothers. Wool embroidery on linen, c. 1070. Musée de la Tapisserie, Bayeux, France.
158. Jack Kerouac, *On the Road*, New York: Signet edition, 1958. Private collection.
159. Evelyn Waugh, *The Ordeal of Gilbert Pinfold. A Conversation Piece*, London: Chapman & Hall, 1957. NNN.10153
161. John Clare, fragment of the poem, *Peasant Poet*, the last 19 verses of *Summer Morning*, early 19th c. Add. 37538 F.
163. Postcard by James Bamforth, from Bamforth's 'songs' series, 1914–18. Pte. Coll.4950/1.
164. H. G. Wells, from *A Modern Utopia*, London, 1909. 12204.d.17/21.
165. Jack London, undated. Library of

Congress, Prints and Photographs Division, Washington, D.C.
166. Margaret Munnerlyn Mitchell with her novel, *Gone with the Wind*, 1937. Alpha Historica/Alamy Stock Photo.
168. André Maurois, *Ariel*, London: Penguin Books, 1935. Private collection.
169. Daniel Defoe in the pillory, wood engraving. Wellcome Collection, London.
170. Pineapple, from *Pomona Britannica*, London: White, Cochrane, and Co, 1812. 10.Tab.41.
172. *Anne Frank's Diary*, written in October 1942. Photo Anne Frank Fonds, Basel via Getty Images.
173. Illustration by T. H. Robinson, from Elizabeth Gaskell's *Cranford*, London: Bliss Sands & Co., 1896. 012621.g.40.
174. Vincent van Gogh, *Self-portrait*, 1889, oil on canvas. Musée d'Orsay, Paris (747).
175. John Evelyn, from *Memoirs Illustrative of the Life and Writings of John Evelyn, Esq., F.R.S*, London: Henry Colburn, 1818. 433.f.13.
177. Peacock Pheasant by George Edwards, from *A Natural History of Uncommon Birds*, London, 1743–51. 435.g.4.(ii).
178. Lord Tennyson by John Tenniel in *Crossing the Bar*, from *Punch or the London charivari*. London, 15 October 1892. C.194.b.199 vol. 103.
179. Philip Larkin, 1974. FG1892-4-14
180. *Nicholas Nickleby*, from *The Works of Charles Dickens*, National edition, London: Chapman & Hall, 1906. Illustration by Hablot Knight Browne (Phiz). 12276.f.1.
182. H. Montgomery Hyde, *The Story of Lamb House Rye: The Home of Henry James*, Rye: Adams of Rye, 1966. X.809/2403.
183. Joseph Conrad, 1923. Ashley 2953*, f.83.
185 (top) Laura Ingalls Wilder, *Little House on the Prairie*, New York; London: Harper & Bros, 1935. Illustration by Helen Sewell. 20054.d.28. (bottom) Louisa M. Alcott, *Little Women*, London: Thomas Nelson & Sons, 1919. YK.1999.b.10183.
186. Fingal's Cave by William Daniell, from *A Voyage Round Great Britain Undertaken in the Summer of the Year 1813*, London: Longman, 1814–25. G.7044 pl. 75.
187. Illustration by Majeska, from *The Picture of Dorian Gray*, New York: Horace Liveright, 1930. Cup.502.e.25.

188. *The English Bible*, London: Doves Press, 1903–05. Image courtesy Heritage Auctions, HA.com.
190. Illustration by Harry Clarke, from *Tales of Mystery and Imagination*, London: G. G. Harrap & Co., 1919. 12703.i.43.
192. Virginia Woolf, *Flush, A Biography*, New York: Harcourt, Brace & Co, 1933. X.329/8532.
194. *Elizabeth I*, woodcut, London: Giles Godhead, 1563. Huth.50.(28).
195. First World War patriotic poster, 1914–19. Tab.11748.a.
196. *View of the River Thames, with Westminster Bridge and Westminster Abbey beyond*, by Joseph C. Stadler, London, 1790. Maps K.Top.22.37.k.
197. Beatrix Potter, *The Tale of Peter Rabbit*, London: Frederick Warne and Co. and New York, 1902. Cup.402.a.4.
198. Goethe, engraving, Leipzig: Philipp Reclam jun., 1949. Library of Congress, Prints and Photographs Division, Washington, D.C.
199. *Album Amicorum of Gervasius Fabricius, of Saltzburg*, 1595–1637. Add MS 17025.
200. Gertrude Stein (right) and Alice B. Toklas in Paris, 1940s. Photo Fotosearch/Getty Images.
202. Alfred Wallis, 'This is Sain Fishery That Used to Be': *St. Ives Harbour and Godrevy Lighthouse*, c. 1930s, oil on board. Barbara Hepworth Museum and Sculpture Garden, St Ives/Bridgeman Images.
203. *View of the bombardment of Fort McHenry, near Baltimore, by the British fleet*, by J. Bower, published c. 1819, re-engraved c. 1905. Library of Congress, Prints and Photographs Division, Washington, D.C.
204. Raymond Chandler, *The Big Sleep*, New York: Alfred A. Knopf, 1939. Private collection.
205. Illustration by Harry Clarke, from Edgar Allan Poe's *Tales of Mystery and Imagination*, London: G. G. Harrap & Co.; New York: Brentano's, 1923. 12703.i.44.
206. Robert Greene, *Greenes Groats-Worth of Witte*, London: Imprinted for William Wright, 1592. C.57.b.42.
207. The death of Caesar in *Julius Caesar*, from *The Works of Shakspere*. Imperial edition, London: J. S. Virtue & Co., 1877. L.R.410.f.7.

208. Snorry Sturluson, *Edda*, 18th c. Icelandic National Library, IB 299 4to, p. 58r.
209. *The death of Sir Philip Sidney at the battle of Zutphen: he passes the water to the soldier*, mezzotint by J. Jones after G. Carter, 1782. Wellcome Collection.
210. (top) *Poetry*, Chicago, October 1912, first issue. Brown University Library, Providence Rhode Island. (bottom) Illustration from *Treasure Island*, London: Cassell & Co, 1883. C.71.c.18.
211. Samuel Johnson and his cat Hodge, from *Chatterbox*, Boston: Estes & Lauriat, 1888. Private collection.
212. Laurence Sterne, from *Het leven en de gevoelens van Tristram Shandy*. Amsteldam: A. E. Munnikhuisen, 1776–79. 1180.a.34.
213. Illustration by H. Sidney in *A Midsummer Night's Dream*, from *Scenes from Shakespeare, for the Young*, London: A. Hays, 1885. 1871.e.4.
214. Illustration from *Robinson Crusoe*, London: Frederick Warne & Co.; New York: Scribner, Welford, & Armstrong, 1872. 12805.l.45.(6).
216. Charlotte Brontë, *Jane Eyre*, London: G. Routledge & Sons, 1889. 12624.f.8, (2.).
218. Dylan Thomas and Caitlin Thomas, late 1930s. Lebrecht Authors/Bridgeman Images.
219. Jules Verne, *Around the World in Eighty Days*, London: Sampson Low, Marston, Searle, & Rivington, 1888. 1608/4408.
220. Washington Irving, from *The Life of George Washington*, New York, 1856–59. 010883.i.2 vol. 1.
221. *Célébrités contemporaines: Emile Zola*, 19th c. Paris Musées/Musée Carnavalet, Histoire de Paris.
222. A representation of the engagement in the Gulf of Lepanto, Oct. 7th 1571, between the combined Spanish and Italian fleets under Don John of Austria and the Turks. Rome, 1571. Maps.C.7.e.2.
223. Illustration by W. W. Denslow, from *The New Wizard of Oz*, Indianapolis: Bobbs-Merrill Co; London: Hodder & Stoughton, 1906. 12813.tt.15.
225. Carel Fabritius, *The Goldfinch*, 1654, oil on panel, Mauritshuis, The Hague.
226. H. G. Wells, *The First Men in the Moon*, London: George Newnes, 1901. Courtesy Heritage Auctions, HA.com.
227. *Prospectus Capitolii Romani cum Scala*

versus Templum Aracaeli, 1750. Bibliothèque nationale de France, département Estampes et photographie (LI-72 (7)-FOL).

228. (top) Thomas Carlyle by Julia Margaret Cameron, 1867. Metropolitan Museum of Art, New York. Alfred Stieglitz Collection, 1949 (49.55.324). (bottom) Poster for Federal Theatre Project presentation of *Uncle Vanya* at the Musart Theatre, Los Angeles, C.A. Library of Congress, Prints and Photographs Division, Washington, D.C.

229. Henry James, *c.* 1910–15. Library of Congress, Prints and Photographs Division, Washington, D.C.

230. The mortal wounding of Admiral Lord Nelson at the sea battle of Trafalgar, 21 October 1805, from *Pictures of English History. From the earliest times to the present period*, London: George Routledge & Sons, 1868. 9595.ff.6.

231. Jane Eyre and Mr. Rochester at Thornfield Hall, from *A Day with Charlotte Brontë*, London: Hodder & Stoughton, 1911. 10601.tt.1/5.

232. *Beowulf, c.* 1000. Cotton Vitellius A. XV, f.132

233. *The cavalry charge at Balaclava, October 25th, 1854, from A Series of 23 coloured lithographic views, representing the principal events during the Russian War*, by W. Simpson and others, from sketches by E. T. Dolby and other artists. London, 1854–55. 1899.b.3.

234. 'Everybody is Talking of the House of Mirth, by Edith Wharton in Scribner's. Are You Reading it?, in *Scribner's*, New York: Charles Scribner's Sons, 1905. Illustration by David Ericson. Library of Congress, Prints and Photographs Division, Washington, D.C.

235. Ballpoint pen advert, 1940s. Private collection.

236. Illustration from *Sense and Sensibility*, London: Macmillan and Co., 1896. 012624.g.5.

238. A scene from *The Woman in White*, from the illustrated music cover, *The Fosco Galop*, London, 1872. h.3174.(15).

240. Jane Austen, *Pride and Prejudice*, London: G. Routledge & Sons, 1883. 12619. aaaa.32.

241. Statue of Liberty, New York. Library of Congress, Prints and Photographs Division, Washington, D.C.

242. (top) Georgette Heyer, *Frederica*, Avon paperback, 1966. Private collection. (bottom) Lewis Carroll, *Through the Looking Glass, And What Alice Found There*, London and New York: Macmillan and Co., 1893. Illustration by John Tenniel. C.194.a.1428.

243. Illustration from *The Adventures of Captain Gulliver, in a Voyage to the Islands of Lilliput and Brobdignag. Abridged from the works of ... Dean Swift. Adorned with cuts*, London: F. Newbery, 1776. Ch.770/46.

244. Illustration by W. Fitzgerald and W. V. Cockburn from Bram Stoker's *Under the Sunset*, London: Sampson Low & Co., 1882. C.194.a.575.

245. A View of the Radcliffe Library, Brazen nose College, the west Front of All Souls College, part of the Schools, a distant View of the Tower of Wadham College, &c. Oxford, 1755. Maps K.Top.34.39.d.

246. Illustration by Majeska, from *The Picture of Dorian Gray*, New York: Horace Liveright, 1930. Cup.502.e.25.

247. Three birds, Golden Plover, by John James Audubon from *The Birds of* America, London, 1827–38. N.L.TAB.2.

249. Illustration by Gustave Doré from *The Rime of the Ancient Mariner*, Leipzig: 1877. 1875.b.5.

250. Fedor Dostoyevsky, *The Idiot*, 1914. Illustration and poem by Sir Philip Sidney. 12206.p.1/506.

251. Sir Walter Raleigh, from *Sir Walter Raleigh's Instructions to his Sonne, and to Posterity*, London: Beniamin Fisher, 1632. C.58.aa.13.

252. *Room in the house of Honoré de Balzac, 17 rue Visconti, Paris*, by Léon Frédéric. Paris Musées/Musée Carnavalet – Histoire de Paris.

253. Herman Melville, *Moby Dick*, New York: Dodd, Mead & Co., 1922. Illustration by Mead Schaeffer. Library of Congress, Washington, D.C.

254. Isabella Bird, from *A Lady's Life in the Rocky Mountains*, London: J. Murray, 1881. 10413.bb.6.

255. Model of The British Library site and building, Euston Road, London. BLSTPancras-02.

256. *Saint Catherine Converting the Scholars*, Flemish, *c.* 1480, oil on panel. The Walters Art Museum, Baltimore, M.D. Gift of Dr. R.

Walter Graham, Jr., 1972 (37.2487).
257. Jean Mallard, Psalter of Henry VIII, illuminated manuscript, 1540. Royal 2 A. XVI.
258. British soldiers fighting in the trenches, from *Newnes Illustrated*, 22 May 1915. c12941-02.
260. Mr Fezziwig's Ball by John Leech, from *A Christmas Carol in Prose. Being a Ghost-Story of Christmas*, London: Chapman & Hall, 1843. C.58.b.7.
263. William Makepeace Thackeray, 1860–69. Library of Congress, Prints and Photographs Division, Washington, D.C.
264. The wreck of the SS *Deutschland*, from *The Sea: its stirring story of adventure, peril & heroism*, vol. 1, p. 652. London: Cassell & Co, 1887. 10498.cc.26.
265. Desdemona by Ludovic Marchetti from *Othello. The Moor of Venice*. London: Simpkin and Co., 1893. 11765.k.9.
266. Sylvia Plath, *Ariel*, London: Faber, 1965. Private collection.
267. Vita, *c.* 1915, from *Vita: The Life of V. Sackville-West*, Harmondsworth: Penguin, 1984. X.958/28500.
268. John Dryden, *The Works of Virgil: containing his Pastorals, Georgics, and Æneis.* Translated into English verse by Mr Dryden, London, 1697. 74.k.10.
269. Illustration from *The Life and Strange Surprising Adventures of Robinson Crusoe*, London: Ernest Nister; New York: E. P. Dutton & Co, 1895. 12604.h.28.

270. Illustration by Cecil Aldin, from *The Posthumous Papers of the Pickwick Club*, London: Chapman & Hall; Lawrence & Jellicoe, 1910. 12612.i.28.
271. Jules Verne, *Le Tour du Monde en quatre-vingts jours*, Paris, 1873. Illustration by M. M. De Neuville and L. Benett. 12514.l.18.
272. Michael Bond by a shop window displaying a Paddington Bear, London, 18 June 1980. Photo United News/Popperfoto via Getty Images/Getty Images.
273. Aphra Behn, from *A Collection of Engraved and Lithographed Portraits of English Poetesses*. England, 1610?–1860?. 1876.f.22.
274. Abbey Theatre program, 1904. Illustration by Elinor Mary Monsell. University of Kansas Libraries.
275. Antoine de Saint-Exupéry, *The Little Prince*, New York: Reynal & Hitchcock, 1943. Private collection.
276. Illustration by Dante Gabriel Rossetti in Christina Georgina Rossetti's *Goblin Market and Other Poems*, London and Cambridge: Macmillan and Co., 1862. Cup.401.b.14.

Cover Images

Main illustration: Border pattern from the title page of *The Story of the Glittery Plain* or *The Land of Living Men*, by William Morris, Hammersmith: Kelmscott Press, 1894. C.43.f.8.
Open book illustration, Shutterstock.

INDEX